High Performance Purchasing

Manufacturing Resource Planning for the Purchasing Professional

High Performance Purchasing

Manufacturing Resource Planning for the Purchasing Professional

John E. Schorr
Thomas F. Wallace

Oliver Wight® Limited Publications, Inc.
5 Oliver Wight Drive
Essex Junction, Vermont 05452

With a great deal of gratitude,
we dedicate this book to

Edna Schorr and Evelyn Wallace

Without their support and encouragement,
it wouldn't have happened.

ISBN: 0-939246-05-8

Printed in the United States of America.
The Book Press, Brattleboro, Vermont.

Table of Contents

Acknowledgments

The authors owe many thanks to many people for making this book possible: our families; our friends and colleagues within the Oliver Wight Companies; and specifically our editor, Bill Farragher; our publisher, Dana Scannell; and our production coordinator, Jennifer Smith.

Also, and perhaps most of all, we're indebted to men and women from a wide spectrum of manufacturing companies in North America and elsewhere. These are companies where it's working, where there truly is a new way of life in purchasing.

These companies have two things in common: They have an excellent MRP/MRP II system, and they're doing an excellent job of sharing the MRP-generated information with their vendors. Our thanks to them for the experiences they've shared with us, and our best wishes for their continued success.

John E. Schorr
Grand Rapids, Michigan
and
Thomas F. Wallace
Cincinnati, Ohio

How to Use This Book

A large part of the audience for this book falls into two categories: first, people in companies implementing Manufacturing Resource Planning (MRP II); and second, purchasing people and other materials professionals interested in expanding their knowledge of these powerful new tools.

In a company implementing MRP II, there will be some people very deeply involved with the specifics of what to do in purchasing and how to do it. They include:

- The purchasing manager.
- The person to whom the purchasing manager reports.
- The buyer and others within the purchasing department.
- The overall MRP II project leader (described in Chapter 5).
- Key people in the areas of planning and scheduling, particularly those who'll be involved with vendor scheduling (described in Chapters 2 and 3).
- Systems and programming people who'll be working closely on the purchasing part of the MRP II system.

We recommend that these people read all chapters in the book. Other people within a company implementing MRP II may wish to learn about MRP II in purchasing, but don't need quite so much input. For them we suggest reading Chapters 1 through 4, and Chapter 8.

The more general reader may wish to read the entire book, and we hope many do. A good alternative is to read Chapters 1,

2, 4, 8, and 9. Then, should interest warrant, the remaining chapters can be read as time is available.

One last point, and it's an important one. To get value from this book, it's essential for the reader to have a general understanding of the structure of MRP II. Those who don't should make it a point to review Appendix A before going beyond the first chapter.

High Performance Purchasing

Manufacturing Resource Planning for the Purchasing Professional

Chapter 1

A New Way of Life in Purchasing

Purchasing people in companies that operate without a Manufacturing Resource Planning (MRP II) system may question the value of such tools. Their position often is: "How will MRP II help me?" The answer to that question is very simple—there's gold in them there hills!

With Manufacturing Resource Planning fully integrated into purchasing, buyers can mine that gold. With MRP II running smoothly, buyers can provide the right material at the right time, keep purchase quantities in line with production needs, and reduce purchased material inventory while simultaneously improving service. In addition, buyers find better communications gives them more time for important tasks like negotiation and value analysis.

Consider the typical manufacturing company:

- For every *one* dollar spent for direct labor, the company spends *three* dollars on direct purchased material.

- The company has a staff of skilled manufacturing engineers, whose job is to develop better methods in manufacturing. They're going after the *one* dollar.

- Who's going after the *three* dollars? In theory, this is the responsibility of the buyers. In practice, few of them can do a totally effective job. Why not? Because they have to spend most of their time expediting vendors and processing paperwork. As a result, enormous opportunities for reduced costs and increased competitiveness can't be pursued.

There is a better way. It ties MRP (Material Requirements Planning) and MRP II (Manufacturing Resource Planning) together with improved methods of communicating a company's requirements to its vendors. First, however, let's take a look at the traditional approach to purchasing and the need to improve upon it.

The Traditional Way of Doing Business

Here's the way most companies have been operating for a long time:

1. The material planner, in the production and inventory control department, determines the need to get more of a purchased item. (The system to make the planner aware of this need may be a manual "perpetual inventory control" technique or a computerized approach of some type, possibly Material Requirements Planning.)

2. The planner sends a written purchase requisition for this item to purchasing. It specifies item number, quantity, and desired due date.

3. The buyer, following receipt of the requisition, prepares a purchase order and sends it to the selected vendor. In effect, the purchase order is a contract that specifies terms, conditions, price, quality, etc., in addition to quantity and date. Copies are also sent to receiving, accounts payable, etc.

4. If the vendor is willing and able to comply, he[1] acknowledges the buyer's order. If not, the vendor typically will respond with an alternative acknowledgment, perhaps specifying different quantities and/or later dates.

[1] People who work in companies can be classified into two general categories: male and female. There is no job category referenced in this book—be it purchasing manager, buyer, vendor scheduler, general manager, vice president, salesperson, foreman, or direct labor person—which in the opinions of these writers cannot be very successfully performed by females. For purposes of simplicity and ease of reading, "he," "him," and "this" will be used throughout the book to refer to a person, be it male or female. Therefore, if it pleases the reader, "he," "him," and "this" can be read as "he or she," "him or her," and "his or hers."

5. In the latter case, the buyer will often need to check with the planner to see if the vendor's alternative plan will support the production schedule. If not, the buyer may need to recontact the vendor to attempt to work out an acceptable compromise.

6. When a good compromise is found, one might think the matter was at an end. Unfortunately, this is not always true. Changes in production schedules often alter requirements for the purchased items. Then, the planner must contact the buyer with a request for change, and the cycle is repeated. As the changes are agreed upon, change order paperwork is created and sent to all those who received copies of the original order. They need to dig into their files, find the original order, put the change order with it, and replace it in the file . . . until the next change order comes through.

What's Wrong with Tradition?

Are there any problems caused by this traditional way of doing business? Yes indeed, quite a few.

Communications are more frequent and complicated than necessary in most companies. Note that, in the above example, the buyer is spending much of his time relaying messages. He doesn't know the details of the demand for the item; only the planner knows that. The buyer doesn't know the specifics of the supply for the item; only the people at the vendor's plant know that. He must talk first to one party, then another, then recontact the first party, etc. In addition to being complex and time-consuming, this approach is also fraught with opportunities for error. At any point, someone may drop the ball and break this delicate communications chain. The probable result: no action, or a decision by default.

Paperwork in this environment can be voluminous. Many purchasing departments spend enormous amounts of time processing requisitions, reviewing and signing purchase orders, matching up acknowledgments, generating change orders, etc.

Expediting typically consumes large amounts of time. Most

companies operate in "order launch and expedite mode." Schedules are invalid and a high percentage of the open purchase orders are past due. The buyer is often forced to spend much of his time expediting just to keep the plant running. Without such efforts, people and equipment would often be idled for lack of parts and material.

Accountability and teamwork between different departments can become very difficult to maintain. A good example is the periodic "inventory reduction program." Due to excessive inventories, management orders production control to cut lot sizes and purchase only the bare minimum needed. At the same time, management hands purchasing a directive to lower purchase costs and improve purchased price variances. Often, this requires buying in large quantities to take advantage of vendor price breaks. Thus, these two departments have been given conflicting objectives. They work at cross-purposes, competing against each other rather than working together against the real competition out in the marketplace.

Lead times quoted by vendors can expand beyond reason. In good times, as an example, we've seen lead times for gray iron castings stretch out to 40 or more weeks. Does it take nine months to produce a casting? A baby—yes; a casting—no. Virtually all of that lead time is backlog. Since the vendor typically has little forward planning information other than the current customer orders, he places new incoming orders at the end of the backlog. Lead time, then, is manufacturing time (usually constant) plus backlog time (variable). When incoming customer orders exceed shipments, backlogs—hence lead times—increase.

Are long lead times bad? Definitely. The longer the lead time, the more uncertain the future need for the item. The risk of obsolescence is greater. Often more safety stock is needed, causing higher inventories. Responsiveness to customer demand can suffer. And long lead times simply aren't necessary. Nor are convoluted communications, mountains of paperwork, continuous expediting, or competing against oneself instead of against the competitors.

Wouldn't It Be Nice If . . .

- vendors could ship the right material at just the right time, routinely?

- purchasing could bring in only quantities that matched production requirements—and not pay more because they didn't buy the larger "price-break" quantity?

- companies could reduce their purchased material inventory sharply and, at the same time, give better service to manufacturing?

- buyers could operate with vendor lead times of three or six or nine weeks, rather than nine months?

- people could work together as a team, and legitimately be held accountable for doing their jobs?

- buyers had time to do the really important parts of their jobs: sourcing, negotiating, contracting, value analysis, working with marginal vendors to make them good ones, and working with good vendors to make them excellent? In other words, time to go after that *three* dollars of purchased material for every *one* dollar of direct labor—to start mining some of that gold?

Well, it really can be done. All of it. It's happening right here in America and in Europe and in Japan. It's happening in companies operating in the following industries:

Computers
Power tools
Automobiles
Oil field equipment
Electronic instrumentation
Clothing
Construction machinery
Diesel engines

Office furniture
Industrial sweepers
Aircraft components
Photocopiers

These companies, whom we know personally, have two things in common: Each has a very good MRP II system, and each is doing an excellent job of using the system-generated information and sharing it with its vendors. Their collective input forms the basis for this book.

A Formal Scheduling System That Works

The only sure thing about life in a manufacturing company is that it'll be different tomorrow. Change is the only constant.

Consider the typical manufacturing facility. Hundreds, perhaps thousands, of people are working on the plant floor. They're operating hundreds, perhaps thousands, of machines which use many sets of tooling. At any one time, there are probably thousands of work orders in process and thousands of purchase orders at vendors.

Murphy's Law states: "Whatever can go wrong, will." If, on a given day, Murphy strikes no more than 1 percent of the time, think of all the things that could go wrong: production that's rejected, customers who change their minds, a third of the work force at home with the flu, broken tooling, mandatory engineering changes, and on and on.

MRP II is a formal system which can cope with change effectively. Unlike other systems, which indicate only "when to order," Material Requirements Planning also routinely tracks "when it's needed." It advises users when the due date of an open production or purchase order no longer matches the need date. For a thorough explanation of Manufacturing Resource Planning, please see Appendix A.

Nowhere is this capability more important than in purchasing.

Demand for direct purchased material, except items purchased for resale, is *dependent*. This demand *depends on and is derived from* the "upstream" production schedules. As production schedules change, so do requirements for purchased items. (*Independent* demand, on the other hand, comes from the marketplace. It impacts on finished goods and service parts.)

Companies that don't have MRP II, or are using it poorly, usually have a difficult time knowing what they really need. Since their formal system can't keep up with change, it's used mainly as an "order launcher." An "informal" system exists side by side with the formal system, and its name is *expediting*.

Most companies (including their purchasing departments, of course) operate in *order launch and expedite* mode. The problems they face as a result include unrealistic schedules, phony backlogs, finger-pointing, little or no real accountability, etc.

A formal planning and scheduling system that works is the foundation of a truly effective purchasing operation. It enables people to answer the fundamental questions: *What do we need and when do we need it.*

The remainder of this book will be devoted to the steps in implementing and using this formal system effectively in purchasing. We will focus on the techniques involved in vendor scheduling, special situations, and measurement techniques, as well as the reorganization necessary to make it all work. Lastly, we'll talk about the very good news of Just-in-Time. We'll discuss why vendor scheduling is a virtual prerequisite for just-in-time purchasing, and how these techniques tie together.

This is *not* a book based on theory or conjecture. The techniques discussed are now being used with great success in purchasing departments around the world. The tools are proven and available. What it takes to make vendor scheduling a reality in a company is the will to make it happen.

Chapter 2
Vendor Scheduling

Think for a moment about what usually happens when a company orders parts or raw materials. The planner requisitions from the buyer. The buyer sends a purchase order to the vendor's sales department. The sales department communicates with the planner in the vendor's plant, as follows:

$$\underline{\text{CUSTOMER}} \qquad \underline{\text{VENDOR}}$$

PLANNER $\longrightarrow$ BUYER $\longrightarrow$ SALES $\longrightarrow$ PLANNER

If a problem arises at the vendor's plant and they're unable to comply, the planner there notifies the salesman, who notifies the buyer, who notifies the planner:

$$\underline{\text{CUSTOMER}} \qquad \underline{\text{VENDOR}}$$

PLANNER $\longleftarrow$ BUYER $\longleftarrow$ SALES $\longleftarrow$ PLANNER

Let's assume the revised promise dates aren't satisfactory and will seriously affect the production schedule. The planner so advises the buyer, who . . . etc., etc., etc.

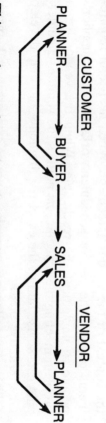

This overly complex and cumbersome communication channel is unnecessary. It's also the method most frequently used in American industry today, simply because it grew up that way.

Back in the days of manual inventory systems, only the people posting the inventory records knew the requirements. It didn't make sense to have the buyers also posting inventory records. The inventory clerks (planners) sent requisitions to the buyers, who did the ordering.

The Vendor Scheduling Concept

With computers and formal systems that work, it's no longer necessary to do it that way. Rather, it becomes a practical matter to put the MRP planning people in direct contact with the vendor. These people are called "vendor schedulers," and they typically communicate directly with scheduling people at the vendor's plant.

In this arrangement, what do the buyers do? The buyers now have the time to do the really important parts of their jobs. Freed from the ongoing pressure of expediting and paperwork, they can concentrate on sourcing, negotiation, contracting, value analysis, etc. See Figure 2-1.

The buyers buy; the vendor schedulers schedule the vendors. In this environment, there is normally a business arrangement, called a "vendor agreement," between the company and the vendor. This agreement, as a rule, is the result of efforts by the buyer (for the company) and the salesman (for the vendor) and, possibly, their managers.

The vendor scheduler enters the picture after the vendor agreement has been finalized. His job is to operate Material Requirements Planning and provide the vendors with schedules within the context of the vendor agreement. When near-term requirements change, the vendor scheduler works with the supplier's people to implement the reschedule. When the vendor has a problem meeting the schedule, he notifies the vendor scheduler, who can advise him of the exact requirements and help develop an alternative plan.

Take the following example, a phone conversation between Jerry (the vendor scheduler) and Sid (Jerry's contact at the supplier's plant):

Communications using vendor scheduling

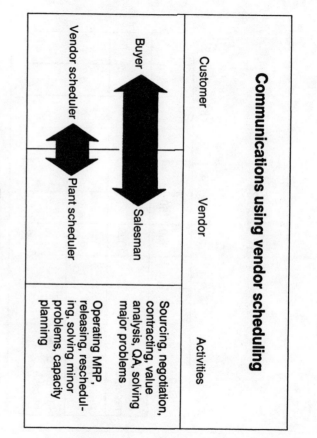

Customer	Vendor	Activities
Buyer	Salesman	Sourcing, negotiation, contracting, value analysis, QA, solving major problems
Vendor scheduler	Plant scheduler	Operating MRP, releasing, rescheduling, solving minor problems, capacity planning

Figure 2-1

SID: Jerry, we've hit a problem running your order for Part #28184.

JERRY: Let's see . . .that's for 1,000 pieces due next Monday, right?

SID: Right. We're less than halfway through the run and the machine went down. It'll take about a week to fix, so I'm afraid we'll be late.

JERRY: Hold on, I'll check MRP.

Jerry checks the MRP display (see Figure 2-2) for Part #28184. He notes the following:

1. There are requirements for 250 in week 2 and 750 one week later.

2. The order ("scheduled receipt") for 1,000 due in week 2 was intended to cover both these requirements.

JERRY: Sid, how many good ones did you get before the problem happened?

SID: 350 for sure, maybe 400.

Part #28184

		Weeks						
	1	2	3	4	5	6	7	8
Proj. gross requirements		250	750					
Scheduled receipts		1000						
Proj. avail. balance	0	0	750	0	0	0	0	0
Planned order release								

Figure 2-2

JERRY: Fine, ship me those. When can you get the rest?

SID: In a week or less.

JERRY: Fine, no problem. How's the family, Sid?

End of conversation. Elapsed time: 30 seconds. Direct, to the point; cooperative, not confrontational. Contrast it with the old way, and here's what would have happened:

Jerry ← Buyer ← Salesman → Sid

Even in the unlikely event all of these communication steps are executed successfully, the buyer has spent valuable time relaying messages. That's time which should have been spent doing the really important parts of his job—the ones that save the company money.

Let's think about paperwork for a minute. What's happened

to the need for written purchase requisitions? Answer: It's disappeared. Requisitions are the traditional common linkage between two people: the person operating the inventory replenishment system (planner), and the person in direct contact with the vendor (buyer). Those two functions are now combined into one person: the vendor scheduler. If the vendor scheduler were to generate a requisition, to whom would he send it? Himself? The answer, of course, is that with vendor scheduling, purchase requisitions with production material simply aren't needed. And as that need disappears, so can hundreds and hundreds of pieces of paperwork.

The Vendor Schedule—Content and Format

A purchase order is simply a contract with a schedule on it. The obvious question is: Why not separate the schedule from the contract?

Why not indeed? Schedules change frequently—every week or so. Contracts change infrequently—perhaps once a year. There's little reason to reissue a new contract every time the schedule changes.

More and more companies are choosing to establish long-term vendor agreements and then issue schedules to them, typically once per week. In general, the buyer develops the vendor agreements, while the vendor scheduler takes care of the schedules. See Figure 2-3.

See Figure 2-4 for a simplified example of a vendor schedule. The different items bought from this vendor are listed vertically on the left side of the chart. Time is expressed in weeks, horizontally. The first four weeks are shown individually; the next four weeks are grouped, as are the following eight weeks.

The quantities shown in the columns are the customer's requirements for the various items. Note the asterisks on the requirements in the first four weeks. These are *firm* requirements. This four-week firm period reflects the vendor's finishing lead time plus an allowance for scheduling time. In this example, the

	Vendor agreement	Vendor schedule
What	Prices, terms, conditions, commitment periods, etc.	Which ones, how many, and when
Who	Buyer and salesman (and/or their managers)	Vendor scheduler and designated person at the vendor's plant (ideally its master scheduler)
How often	Normally every year or two. Possibly open-ended	About once per week

Figure 2-3

vendor agreement (not shown) specifies a four-week firm horizon, which means:

1. The vendor is required to ship according to this schedule.

2. The company cannot change the quantity or timing of these requirements without approval from the vendor inside the four-week window.

3. The vendor is authorized to produce any of these firmed-up requirements early and hold them in his inventory until time to ship. The company is obligated to take them, but not sooner than the schedule specifies. In this manner, the vendor is able to group production runs to achieve internal efficiencies. The company receives shipments in quantities which directly match his production requirements and, if he chooses, on a "Just-in-Time" basis.

To take this example further, the vendor agreement might also specify that requirements in the second four-week period represent a commitment to cover the vendor for any material unique to that customer. In other words, the vendor is authorized to purchase special material for these requirements. If the company's requirements are eliminated for all items using a special or unique material, the company may have agreed to protect the vendor

Jones Company vendor schedule for: Smith, Inc.

Part #	Week: 1	2	3	4	5-8	9-16
13579	100*			100	200	
24680	20	20*	20*	20*	80	160
42457	300*		200*	800	1600	
77543			40*	40	40	

*Firm

Figure 2-4

from being stuck with obsolete stock. This could be done, if necessary, by paying the vendor's restocking charge from his supplier or, worst case, directly reimbursing the vendor for his costs of the material.

The column farthest to the right, weeks 9–16, is for information only, and there is no company commitment at all. It's there mainly to help the vendor plan his resources—people, equipment, tooling, money, etc.

Benefits

What are the typical benefits of this approach? They're both numerous and significant:

- *Low inventories.* Manufacturers can get just the amount they need, just when they need it.

- *Low prices.* Buyers have negotiated pricing in advance, across the board. They've asked the vendor for his best prices on the entire volume of business and no longer need to be concerned with the details of his traditional pricing structure on a given item for a specific order.

- *"Price breaks"* in the traditional sense are not as significant as before. Price breaks exist largely to enable the vendor to run a larger quantity at one time, in order to amortize the setup costs over a larger quantity.

The information and visibility contained within the vendor schedule gives the vendor a far better opportunity for cost reduction and efficiencies, via techniques such as combining runs, sequencing runs to minimize changeover time, etc. It then becomes the buyer's job to ensure the vendor passes on a good percentage of these savings. The vendor benefits, and so does the company.

• *Constant pricing.* Another result, in addition to lower prices, is constant pricing over a longer period of time. Price increases based on "price at time of shipment" are "surprises" that most buyers like to avoid. Since the vendor is authorized to acquire material out into the future with vendor scheduling, price increases based on rises in his material costs should be sharply reduced in the near term.

If the vendor's labor costs are scheduled to increase, the company may wish to authorize him to run the entire schedule prior to the increase, but to ship the material as needed. Again, this gives the company constant pricing over the life of the schedule.

• *Short lead times.* As we said earlier, most of a vendor's lead time is often made up of backlog. As the backlog increases, so do the quoted lead times. However, with vendor scheduling, quoted lead times aren't nearly as important. The vendor schedule extends out into the future, well beyond the vendor's quoted lead times. This is a "win-win" situation. The vendor has more and better information on which to plan, and the company is freed from issuing purchase orders for specific items in specific quantities far into the future.

With vendor scheduling, the most important vendor lead time is the finishing lead time. This is never more than the complete manufacturing time, and is almost always less than the "quoted lead time." It represents the point of commitment to specific finished items. This finishing lead time, plus perhaps a week or so for the vendor's internal scheduling, establishes the "firm zone" on the vendor schedule. In the example shown in Figure 2-4, this zone is the first four weeks.

All quantities shown within that period are firm. The vendor scheduler resists making changes in this zone, and vendor concurrence is required prior to making a change. Thus the vendor is assured of stability in his schedule, and the company receives the benefits of shorter lead times.

In some customer-vendor arrangements, the second time zone—four weeks in this example—might be considered a "trade-off zone." In this period, the level of volume would be considered as set, but changes could be made to the quantity and timing of individual orders. In the "open zone"—weeks 9–16—the ability to make changes would be relatively open.

Note the similarity between this and the standard approach to Master Production Scheduling. Time fences define a firm zone, a trade-off zone, and an open zone. As more companies implement MRP II, we predict much greater attention will be paid to the time fences in the vendor's master scheduling policy than to the vendor's quoted lead times.

• *Less paperwork.* With vendor schedules, individual purchase orders are no longer needed. Some companies have retained purchase order *numbers* for administrative reasons, while eliminating individual purchase orders.

This reduction in purchase order paperwork can be substantial. This is in addition to a comparable reduction resulting from the elimination of purchase requisitions, as discussed earlier. It all means substantially more time for the buyers to do the really important parts of their jobs by getting out of the constant paperwork and expediting hassle.

A more detailed example of a vendor schedule is shown in Figure 2-5. It shows the following:

• The company's name, the vendor's name, the vendor number, the date, and the initials of the vendor scheduler and the buyer.

• The first six columns show weekly data, the seventh shows a four-week accumulation, and the eighth shows a twelve-week

Vendor #114

Jones Company vendor schedule for: Smith, Inc. — week of 02/01/8X

Vendor Scheduler: AB
Buyer: CD

Firm Zone: first 04 weeks

Material Zone: next 06 weeks

-- Requirements --

FFFFFFFFFFFFFFFFFFFFFFFFFFFFFFFFFFFF MMMMMMMMMMMMMMMMMM

Item #	Description		Week 2/1 & previous	Week 2/8	Week 2/15	Week 2/22	Week 3/01	Week 3/08	Next 04 Wks	Next 12 Wks
13579	Plate	Qty:		100				100	100	300
		PO#:		B1146						
24680	Panel	Qty:	20	20	20	20	20	20	80	340
		PO#:	B1122	B1146	B1180	B1203				
42457	Tube	Qty:	300			200			1100	3500
		PO#:	B1122			B1203				
77543	Frame	Qty:			40		40			
		PO#:			B1180					

Figure 2-5

accumulation. Thus, the vendor in this case is provided with 22 weeks of forward visibility. If necessary, more could be provided by merely increasing the number of weeks in the columns farthest to the right. The key is giving visibility to the vendor *well beyond* his quoted lead times.

• The firm time fence is set at four weeks into the future. This is indicated in several ways:

1. It's spelled out in the header information.

2. The letter "F," indicating "firm," is shown above the dates for the first four weeks.

3. All required quantities in the first four weeks carry a purchase order number below them. In this example, the company has elected to retain purchase order numbers for administrative reasons, even though they've eliminated individual purchase order paperwork.

This issue of whether or not purchase orders are necessary can be an emotional one in some companies. The facts are that individual *hard-copy purchase orders are not necessary*, but purchase order *numbers* may be needed for control purposes.

One method to accomplish this is shown in Figure 2-5, as we've seen. An alternative method would be to use the item number and due date. Thus, the first item would have a purchase order number of 13579-0208. A third alternative: vendor number and due date. This would show all quantities in a given week under one number, for example 114-0208.

Companies not requiring purchase order numbers would probably print an asterisk next to the requirement to indicate the order is firm, as shown earlier in Figure 2-4.

The Degree of Future Commitment

Questions sometimes arise regarding the degree of commitment to the vendors involved in vendor scheduling. In other words, does a company find itself making firm commitments further into the future with vendor scheduling than with conventional purchase orders? Or further than with blanket orders? Or further than with "buying capacity"?

In each of these cases, the answer is no. Vendor scheduling, done properly, results in a *reduced* firm future commitment. Let's examine the alternatives:

• Conventional purchase orders require commitments to specific items, quantities, and timing out through the vendor's total lead time. Of course, this includes his "backlog" time. Vendor scheduling keys on the vendor's true manufacturing time and firms up only those orders within that period. Since these times are shorter, the commitment period is correspondingly smaller.

• Blanket orders typically require a commitment to the vendor for a specific quantity (or perhaps quantity range) of a specific item over an extended time into the future—often at a predetermined delivery schedule. In vendor scheduling, there is no long-term commitment to specific quantities and timing.

• Buying capacity usually means committing to the vendor for a given level of volume per time period over an extended time into the future. With vendor scheduling, there is normally no such firm commitment. There are situations, however, when good vendor scheduling requires capacity buying, and we'll discuss these in Chapter 4.

Multiple-Sourcing

Vendor scheduling does not require sole-sourcing. Most of the companies using it today are multiple-sourced in significant ways. However, many of them do a great deal of sole-sourcing, and there is a definite trend toward reducing the number of suppliers.

Good software for vendor scheduling makes multiple-sourcing more practical. With good software, the vendor scheduler is able to specify the share of an item's total requirements for Vendor A, Vendor B, etc. and the vendor schedules reflect this split. (The vendor scheduler is typically not a decision maker in this matter of apportioning volume to various vendors but executes decisions made by the buyer or the purchasing manager.) Some companies show the vendors the total volume on the item as well as their share of it. This can serve as an incentive for each of them to do a better job and gain a greater share of the business.

In any case, the best companies work very closely with their vendors. Communication is frequent and open. The schedules are valid, so the dates are believable. The vendor knows the customer's environment, problems, and opportunities—and vice versa. Mutual trust is recognized as important and is nourished. The vendors are looked upon as "part of the team."

As shown in Figure 2-5, the company is now able to provide the vendor with information to help him plan his future workloads. The information in the rightmost column contains requirements for weeks 11 through 22. The company's not committed for these quantities; they're just forecasts.

Why Help the Vendor?

Sometimes people question why they should help their vendor plan his capacity needs. Their attitude is: "It's not our problem." Well, one important reason to help the vendor is that, without this "forecast" information, he will be forced to guess at the customer's future needs. Then the customer will have to rely on the quality of the vendor's guess rather than on the quality of the planned orders in the MRP II system. In rising markets, customers often find themselves put on allocation when the vendor "guessed wrong." The issue is not "to forecast or not to forecast," but merely "who forecasts."

Giving better information to vendors enhances their ability to give customers what they need, when they need it. Many companies using vendor scheduling have found high-quality information helps mediocre vendors become good ones, and good ones become excellent. Their philosophy is: "Let's help them to help us. Their problems are our problems."

Enhancements to the Vendor Schedule— Capacity Planning

Figure 2-6 is an example of a vendor schedule enhanced by additional capacity planning information. A "capacity unit of measure" has been added to the right of the item description, for use when a customer is buying a variety of different items from a vendor. Let's assume these items consume varying amounts of capacity in the vendor plant. In this situation, the vendor can't merely add up the requirements in pieces for a given period and get a meaningful measure of workload.

The capacity unit of measure "translates" piece part requirements into capacity requirements meaningful to the vendor. In Figure 2-6, for example, Part #13579 has a capacity value of 2.5. Therefore, the 100-piece requirement in the week of 2/8 translates to a capacity requirement of 250 for that week.

The other items shown require different amounts of capacity, the units of measure for which are shown. As with the first item, these are used to translate piece part requirements into vendor capacity terms. For example, the 20-piece requirement for Part #24680 in the current week and beyond is shown as 200 units of vendor capacity. Similar calculations are shown for the other items.

The resulting capacity requirements are totaled and shown at the bottom. For columns containing more than one week, a weekly average is shown. (This information points out a potential problem with this vendor, which we'll discuss later in this chapter.)

How does the company obtain these capacity units of measure? By asking the vendor. He knows where his bottleneck operations are and the capacity terms in which he thinks of them. Further, given the necessary education and training about MRP II and vendor scheduling, he'll usually be more than glad to provide them. Some typical examples of vendors' capacity units of measure are shown in Figure 2-7.

Jones Company vendor schedule for: Smith, Inc. — week of 02/01/8X

Vendor Scheduler: AB   Firm zone: first 04 weeks   Material zone: next 06 weeks
Buyer: CD

-- Requirements --
FFFFFFFFFFFFFFFFFFFFFFFFFFFFFFFFFFFFFFFF   MMMMMMMMMMMMMMMMMMMM

Item #	Descr.	Cap. u/m		Week 2/1 & previous	Week 2/8	Week 2/15	Week 2/22	Week 3/01	Week 3/08	Next 04 Wks	Next 12 Wks
13579	Plate		Qty.:		100				100	100	300
			P.O.#:		B1146						
		2.5	Cap.:		250				250	250	750
24680	Panel		Qty.:	20	20	20	20	20	20	80	340
			P.O.#:	B1122	B1146	B1180	B1203				
		10.0	Cap.:	200	200	200	200	200	200	800	3400
42457	Tube		Qty.:	300			200			1100	3500
			P.O.#:	B1122			B1203				
		1.0	Cap.:	300			200			1100	3500
77543	Frame		Qty.:			40		40			
			P.O.#:			B1180					
		3.0	Cap.:			120		120			
Total capacity requirements:				500	450	320	400	320	450	2150	7650
Weekly average:									536	538	638

Figure 2-6

Examples of vendor capacity units of measure

Commodity	Customer Unit of measure	Vendor Unit of measure
Castings	Each	Molds, trees
Forgings	Each	Hammer strokes
Sheet metal	Square feet	Pounds
Cartons	Each	Square feet
Liquids	Pints, quarts, gallons	Liters

Figure 2-7

Some vendors have required this type of "translation" into their own internal unit of measure for a long time. One example is sheet metal. Often the purchasing company's unit of measure is square feet. The bills of material are expressed that way, and the material is inventoried and issued in square feet. However, the vendor's unit of measure is pounds, and he wants his information in that manner. This translation can be awkward, particularly in purchasing and receiving.

The capacity unit of measure on the vendor schedule can ease this situation. In the sheet metal example, the "Qty" row could show square feet (the company's unit of measure) while the "Cap" row could show pounds (the vendor's unit of measure).

This display of information is also useful when future requirements are changing. The rightmost column of requirements, captioned "Next 12 weeks," shows an average weekly requirement of over 638 units (in capacity terms). This is substantially in excess of the customer's requirements now and in the recent past. It's also substantially in excess of the vendor's current level of output, which is closely matching current requirements. Again, this type of information should raise a flag to the buyer, the vendor scheduler, and the vendor personnel. Obvious questions arise:

1. Given the vendor's current situation, can he supply the customer at this higher level of volume easily?

2. If not, what changes can be made in his plant to enable him to do so?

3. Is the vendor willing and able to make these changes?

4. If not, can the company "offload" some of this volume to another vendor?

Seeing these kinds of potential problems ahead of time can make a big difference. It can enable buyers and their vendors to anticipate problems, rather than being forced to routinely react to them.

Enhancements to the Vendor Schedule—Input/Output Control

In an MRP II system, one of the key elements is feedback, or tracking performance to the plan. For the "inside factory"—one's own shop—the technique used to track capacity performance to plan is called input/output control. Standard hours of actual output for each work center are compared to its planned output. (The same is true for input to each work center, to ensure the work is actually there.) Deviations of actual performance to plan are calculated. When the cumulative deviation exceeds a predetermined tolerance limit, corrective action is taken.

A similar approach can be taken for the "outside factories," that is, a company's vendors. Figure 2-8 shows an example of a vendor schedule with vendor performance information added.

This information is shown at the bottom, in the area labeled "Performance summary." In this example, prior weeks' requirements are expressed in capacity terms—"Capacity units required"—as are receipts, so an "apples-to-apples" comparison can be made. The Cumulative deviation line represents the running comparison of actual to plan. A cumulative deviation that increases beyond a predetermined tolerance limit would be a signal to the buyer, vendor scheduler, and vendor personnel that corrective action must be taken.

The last line shows deliveries missed by the vendor. This highlights vendor performance to *specific deliveries*, as opposed to performance to the overall plan.

Vendor #114

Jones Company vendor schedule for: Smith, Inc. — week of 02/01/8X

Vendor Scheduler: AB   Firm Zone: first 04 weeks   Material Zone: next 06 weeks
Buyer: CD

-- Requirements --
*FFFFFFFFFFFFFFFFFFFFFFFFFFFFFFFFFFFFFFFF*MMMMMMMMMMMMMMMMMMMM

Item #	Descr.	Cap. u/m		Current + Past due	Week 2/8	Week 2/15	Week 2/22	Week 3/01	Week 3/08	Next 04 wks.	Next 12 wks.
13579	Plate	2.5	Qty.:		100				100	100	300
			P.O.#:		B1146						
			Cap.:		250				250	250	750
24680	Panel	10.0	Qty.:	20	20	20	20	20	20	80	340
			P.O.#:	B1122	B1146	B1180	B1203				
			Cap.:	200	200	200	200	200	200	800	3400
42457	Tube	1.0	Qty.:	300			200			1100	3500
			P.O.#:	B1122			B1203				
			Cap.:	300			200			1100	3500
77543	Frame	3.0	Qty.:			40		40			
			P.O.#:			B1180					
			Cap.:			120		120			
Total capacity requirements:				500	450	320	400	320	450	2150	7650
Weekly average:									536	538	638

Performance summary-prior wks.	Last wk	2 wks ago	3 wks ago	4 wks ago	4-wk tot.	*Ytd.	Volume	%
Capacity units required:	580	495	520	565	2160		22427	
Received:	582	580	406	573	2141		22298	
Cumulative deviation:	2	87	-27	-19	-19		-129	-0.1
Deliveries missed:	0	0	1	0	1			10.0

Figure 2-8

The information in the two columns farthest to the right on the bottom of Figure 2-8 indicates that the vendor's volume performance year-to-date is very good, over 99 percent. However, he has missed 10 percent of his planned deliveries, which would normally be considered unacceptable.

Currently, we're not aware of any companies doing input/output control formally for their vendors. However, it certainly makes sense and, in many situations, would be a very valuable tool. It's included here as a logical extension of vendor scheduling.

Consider the similarities between information for the "inside factory" (the company's plant) and the "outside factory" (their vendors' plants):

1. With MRP II, companies can give their plant realistic, valid, attainable schedules of what to produce and when. They can do the same thing for their vendors.

2. With MRP II, companies can do capacity requirements planning for their own plant. They can also do it for their vendors.

3. With MRP II, companies can track input/output performance for their own plant. They can also do it for their vendors.

4. Since the schedules are valid, the plants operate on the principle of "silence is approval." This means that, as long as they will hit the schedule, nothing needs be said. When something goes wrong to cause a missed schedule, then they need to give feedback.

With vendor scheduling companies can ask the same thing of their vendors. In companies doing vendor scheduling well, routine "follow-ups" of vendors have become a thing of the past. Vendors know that the due dates are valid. They know the company needs the items at those times. When a vendor has a problem and can't ship on time, he knows it's necessary to notify the company *at once.* Otherwise, he says nothing and ships on time. Silence is approval.

Chapter 3
Organizing for Vendor Scheduling

In Chapter 2, we discussed the techniques involved in doing vendor scheduling. Here we will cover the organizational changes necessary to permit a company to use these techniques effectively.

The Traditional Method

As we saw earlier, most companies have a planner who determines the needs for purchased items. He enters the quantity and due date on a requisition and forwards it to purchasing. Upon receipt of the requisition, and barring any difficulties, the buyer creates the purchase order. The typical structure of such an organization is shown in Figure 3-1.

Unfortunately, in many companies, the planner and buyer do not work well together. The reason is easy to understand. The planner is normally held accountable for the dollars in inventory and, therefore, tends to requisition smaller quantities to keep the inventory low. On the other hand, the buyer is accountable for price. He'll tend to work toward getting the largest quantity price break possible. If he's unable to get the maximum price break, he may go back to the planner and ask him to increase the order

Organization		
Traditional	Planner writes requisitions	Buyer places orders

Figure 3-1

quantity. Perhaps without realizing it, the company has set conflicting goals for these two functions.

There's another problem, as well. Without a valid planning and scheduling system, the initial due dates on requisitions may be incorrect; they may not reflect when the material is really needed in the plant. In addition, due to constantly changing priorities in the factory, it can be very difficult for the due dates to be *kept* valid during the life of an order.

In this environment, the buyer doesn't really know when the orders are needed. If a company runs out before the shipment from the vendor arrives, the finger-pointing begins. The planner blames the buyer for not respecting the dates on his requisitions. In return, the buyer accuses the planner of giving him incorrect need dates.

In most companies the planners are not allowed to talk to the vendors, and there are several reasons for this. The first concerns the due date. Since purchasing people feel they don't get valid dates on the requisitions from the planners, they don't want the planners passing these unrealistic dates on to the vendors. Purchasing also fears the planners may treat the vendors unfairly, violating lead times or perhaps minimum order quantities. In other words, they're concerned the planners may break down the rapport the buyer has worked so hard to establish with his vendors. Second, the planners in most companies are organized by product lines, not commodities. Therefore, two or more planners could possibly contact a vendor at the same time, giving him conflicting priorities.

The Combined Method

As industry made the transition from manual to computerized inventory recordkeeping, some opportunities opened up. As the recordkeeping became less time-consuming, it became practical to allow one person, typically a buyer, to do both the buying and the planning (see Figure 3-2). That person is often called a buyer/planner.

Under this combined form of organization, the buyer/planner receives computer-generated information on each of his purchased items. He reviews this output, reacting to the action messages on each item as needed. Once this planning is complete, he places the purchase orders with the vendor and performs all the normal purchasing functions.

This approach gives the buyer/planner much better information than before. He can see the need dates on every item and can easily increase order quantities or combine items to get the price breaks desired. He's freed of requisition paperwork, so the paperwork burden is reduced. Further, with an effective MRP II system in place, the dates can be kept valid, thus sharply reducing the buyer's expediting workload.

It's not all good news, however. The buyer now has to do the planning in addition to his buying responsibilities. Some, possibly much, of the time freed up by less paperwork and better dates now must be devoted to the planning function. There can remain the classic problem of insufficient time for the buyers to do the really important parts of their jobs—sourcing, negotiation, value analysis, etc.

The Vendor Scheduler Method

As a result, some very forward-thinking purchasing departments found a better way. Since MRP II can generate and maintain valid need dates, much of the traditional conflict between the buyer and planner can be eliminated. Planners can now be organized by commodity and can work directly with the vendor on details

---

Organization		
Traditional	Planner writes requisitions	Buyer places orders
Combined	Buyer (Buyer/Planner) plans and also orders	

Figure 3-2

of the schedule. Often, they're given a new title: vendor scheduler. The buyer's job now changes to what it should have been all along: spending money well.

This new organizational structure is shown at the bottom of the Figure 3-3.

	Organization	
Traditional	Planner writes requisitions	Buyer places orders
Combined	Buyer/Planner plans and also orders	
Vendor Scheduler	Vendor scheduler plans and orders	Buyer negotiates contracts, solves major problems, etc.

Figure 3-3

Please be aware than it's not necessary to go through the combined method to get to vendor scheduling. We recommend that a company go right to vendor scheduling from whatever its current arrangement may be, and we'll expand on this in Chapter 6.

The Vendor Scheduler's Job

What does the vendor scheduler do? First, he analyzes the material requirements planning reports and reacts to the messages out of the system. The types of messages he would review include:

- Release an order.
- Reschedule an order in.
- Reschedule an order out.
- Cancel an order.
- Resolve data problems.

Material Requirements Planning looks out into the future and calculates when the company will need to receive more material from its vendors on each purchased item. It offsets by the vendor's lead time and recommends when to place an order. This is called a "planned order" because it is only a recommendation from the system. As time passes, that planned order release moves from, for example, week 4 to week 3, from week 3 to week 2, from week 2 to week 1. When it gets into week 1, the Material Requirements Planning system gives the vendor scheduler a message to firm up that order with the vendor. The vendor scheduler then converts that planned order to a "scheduled receipt," which authorizes the selected vendor to produce the item. If there is a problem from the vendor's viewpoint, the buyer may need to get involved and resolve the problem prior to the placement of the order.

Material Requirements Planning is also constantly reviewing the need date (when the first piece is needed) against the due date (when the vendor has been asked to deliver the item). If the need date changes, either in or out, the system gives the vendor scheduler a message to move the due date accordingly (reschedule in or reschedule out). The vendor scheduler contacts the vendor and requests the change in due date. If the vendor agrees to the change, there's no problem. The scheduled receipt's due date on the computer is simply changed to reflect the new date. If the vendor cannot or will not change the date, the vendor scheduler may contact the buyer, who tries to resolve the differences.

On occasion, the system will also recommend canceling an order with a vendor. This can happen when a customer has canceled an order and the manufacturer no longer needs a scheduled purchased item. In these cases, the vendor scheduler contacts the vendor to try to cancel the order. If there are no problems, the order is canceled. If there are problems, perhaps cost implications, the buyer would need to get involved and negotiate the necessary settlement.

The system will also generate messages to indicate data problems. A good example of this would be the vendor's weekly capacity. Consider a vendor that works five days a week, eight hours a day, on one purchased item. The vendor can produce 10,000 parts in a typical week. This maximum of 10,000 parts would be input into the system. Suppose business picks up, and the manufacturer needs 11,000 of that item in a particular week. The system would give the planner a message saying in effect, "This exceeds the vendor's stated capacity." The planner would contact the vendor and either get the vendor's agreement to produce the larger quantity or perhaps pull part of the 11,000 quantity into the previous week. If this is a problem for the vendor or a cost is involved, the vendor scheduler would once again involve the buyer to resolve the situation.

In short, the vendor scheduler does all the planning via MRP, handling the 90 to 95 percent of the items that are routine. The few exceptions are handled by the buyer. The buyer, now freed of all the traditional paperwork and routine replenishment planning, has the time to really do his job of buying well.

The second area of responsibility of the vendor scheduler is to maintain the information in the system. If a price changes or the buyer negotiates a new lead time or selects a new vendor, the buyer passes the information on to the vendor scheduler, who inputs it into the system. After verifying that the master data is correct, he lets the buyer know that the change has been completed. This allows the buyer to exercise management control over the Material Requirements Planning system, but frees him of actually having to do the time-consuming transactions himself.

The third area of responsibility of the vendor scheduler is to respond to changes to the schedule, to engineering changes, and to vendor delivery problems. "Can the vendor move the shipment of parts from Thursday to Monday?" "Can he give us the red ones before the blue ones?" "We just broke the tool. Tell the vendor we won't need the half inch size until next week. What size can he move up sooner?" The vendor scheduler becomes the eyes and ears of both the vendor and the shop.

The last area of responsibility of the vendor scheduler concerns the actual generation of the vendor schedules. After all the necessary planned orders have been converted into scheduled receipts in the Material Requirements Planning system, all the reschedule messages completed, and all the changes updated, the system can then be authorized to generate the vendor schedule. The vendor scheduler is responsible for transmitting the weekly schedule to the vendor. He may also check with the vendor to ensure receipt of the schedule and that it is practical and attainable.

The Buyer's Job

The vendor scheduler has freed the buyer of the paperwork associated with requisitions and purchase orders and taken on the bulk of the day-to-day contact with the vendor. Now the buyer can do his job: spend money well. His full-time job becomes value analysis, negotiation, vendor selection, alternate-sourcing, quality negotiation, and lead time negotiation. He has time to sit down with engineering to understand the function of an item and its critical elements (tolerances, specifications, etc.). He has new opportunities to work with vendors to find ways to satisfy the function of the item at a lower cost. There's time to do effective negotiation on all the items, not just the high-ticket ones.

Appendix B details a recent survey of successful users of Manufacturing Resource Planning, focusing on their results in purchasing. In this survey, the companies using vendor schedulers reported an average 11 percent annual purchase cost reduction. Why? We believe it's primarily because the buyers had the time to do their jobs (in addition, of course, to furnishing the vendors with valid schedules generated by MRP). Those companies having buyer/planners reported an average 7 percent annual cost reduction. Why the difference? Under the buyer/planner concept, the buyer has to spend time doing the planning and follow-up function. That takes time away from value analysis, negotiation, etc. Under vendor scheduling, the buyer's full-time job is getting the best return on the money he has to spend.

Buyers also have the time for vendor selection. As we'll discuss in Chapter 7, they can use vendor measurement reports to evaluate how well the vendor is performing. There's time to search out alternative sources, either to assure supply or to replace a vendor that isn't performing up to expectations. They have the opportunity to negotiate quality and resolve differences between the vendor's specifications and their own. Quality measurement reports identify the parts below quality standards. Buyers have time to then work with the vendors to install statistical process quality control. There's time to work with engineering on tolerances, to help them with standardization programs and thereby improve incoming quality.

Lead times can be negotiated more easily as well. By visiting the vendor's plants, the buyer can determine the real elements of lead times at the vendor's plant. He can get answers to such questions as: When does the vendor need to order raw materials? When does the vendor set aside capacity to make the parts? How long does it actually take to produce the item? By using the vendor schedule to forecast raw material and capacity needs, the buyer can negotiate a shorter lead time based upon the vendor's actual manufacturing time. In short, the buyer is given the time to do *all* the functions of his job well. Since he's now an expert at buying, rather than paperwork and expediting, he can become a highly motivated, contributing professional in the purchasing department.

A Potential Dilemma

To whom should the vendor schedulers report? The purchasing manager may feel that the vendor schedulers should report to him, since they're in direct contact with his vendors. The manager of production and inventory control might want the vendor schedulers reporting to him, since they're operating MRP. What's the solution to this potential dilemma?

The answer gets down to the basic issue of accountability. We feel that the vendor scheduling function should report to that manager who has accountability for the *performance of the purchased material inventory*. Inventory performance in this context means two things: service and turnover.

- *Service*—to manufacturing and to the customers. This means keeping manufacturing supplied with purchased items so it can operate efficiently and without interruption, and it means providing good customer service on purchased spares and finished goods.

- *Turnover*—keeping the inventory levels low.

The manager who can best be held accountable for this purchased inventory performance is the logical choice to manage the vendor scheduling operation. In some companies, this might be the purchasing manager; in others the production control manager, or perhaps the materials manager, could be the best choice.

All things being equal, we recommend that the vendor scheduling group be a part of the purchasing department. In this arrangement, there's only one person to consult if there is a purchased item problem—the purchasing manager. It makes no difference if the item was ordered too late, if the vendor didn't ship on time, if the quantity is wrong, if the inventory level is incorrect on a purchased item, etc. The purchasing manager is ultimately responsible for all purchased item problems. If the vendor scheduler reports to production and inventory control, there may be confusion on who to call—the purchasing manager or the production and inventory control manager.

Also, if the vendor scheduler reports to production and inventory control, there may remain some conflict between order quantity and price breaks. If the vendor scheduler reports to purchasing, the purchasing manager is held accountable to manage pricing while staying below his total inventory dollar limit.

That's the theory. In actual practice, it really doesn't seem to matter very much. In the survey mentioned earlier, about half of the companies had the vendor schedulers as part of the purchasing department, and roughly half had them in production and inventory control.

In most companies, regardless of reporting structure, the vendor schedulers sit in close proximity to the purchasing department. In this way, the vendor schedulers can easily update buyers on potential problems as they occur. In return, the buyers keep the vendor schedulers informed on key issues.

Quality problems can be handled jointly by the buyer and vendor scheduler. The vendor scheduler needs to get a replacement shipment, while the buyer needs to resolve the underlying reason for the quality problem. The buyer also needs to keep the vendor scheduler up to date on pricing and lot size changes, so he can input the data, and replan as necessary.

The vendor scheduler keeps the buyer updated on engineering changes and new product timing so he can select vendors and negotiate pricing prior to the effectivity date.

The buyer informs the vendor scheduler about pending changes in vendors, new vendors, etc. This can enable the vendor scheduler to help the new vendor with material and capacity planning information, and to begin to build the relationship.

In short, the buyer and vendor scheduler work together to resolve problems and handle changes before they can cause a production shortage. When a vendor calls to discuss quality or pricing, he sees the buyer. When he calls to discuss delivery, he sees the vendor scheduler. But because they work as a team, often both the buyer and vendor scheduler together will meet with the vendor to be sure all bases are covered before the vendor leaves. Anything short of a team effort may cause a return to the old "your vendor, your schedule" finger-pointing routine, hot lists, and less-than-desired results.

How many vendor schedulers will a company need? Our survey showed an average of one vendor scheduler supporting two buyers. Since the buyers and vendor schedulers are set up on a commodity basis, it is fairly easy to arrange the commodities so this 2:1 ratio can work smoothly.

A question arises: Will we need to hire more people in order to staff the vendor scheduling function? The answer is almost always no. The vendor schedulers can often be drawn from the existing planner group, as a result of reassigning planning responsibilities from a product orientation to a commodity orientation on the purchased items.

Materials Management

In many companies today, purchasing, production and inventory control, and other departments report to a person called the materials manager. His job is to coordinate and resolve the problems that can occur between the various materials departments. Purchasing wants larger lot sizes. Production and inventory control wants smaller lot sizes. Traffic wants truckload shipments. The warehouse wants even flow of material, etc.

With MRP II, the company now has valid priorities, and many of the problems encountered with the informal system disappear. Hot lists disappear, expediting is dramatically reduced, inventory is lowered, weekly or smaller shipments of purchased items even the flow of material. Traffic is provided with advanced schedules of inbound freight with which to negotiate freight rates.

Therefore, much of the need for a "referee" is removed. The vendor schedulers are given the responsibility of scheduling purchased items and staying within their inventory target; the production schedulers are given the responsibility of scheduling work-in-process and staying within their inventory target. Therefore, in many MRP II companies, the need for the materials management form of organization is lessened. Or as our friend Jim Burlingame, Executive Vice President, Twin-Disc, Inc., says, "You don't need materials management to manage your materials."

Multi-Plant Operations

Many companies today have multiple plant operations. They often have a central purchasing department but their manufacturing operations are decentralized. Typically, each operation does its own production scheduling and generates its own material requirements, then forwards them to a central buying group to be purchased. Normally, they would come to purchasing on a requisition of some type, rather than as a material requirements planning output, which makes it impossible for purchasing to do vendor scheduling.

There are two approaches to this problem. If each plant has its own computer and its own MRP II software, then the vendor scheduling function can be located at the plant site. Central purchasing can be supplied with the annual quantities of all the parts used at all the facilities and would do annual contracting, based upon the total combined requirements for each item. Once the vendor is selected, and the terms or conditions negotiated, the vendor scheduling function at the plant site would do all of the vendor scheduling. Though they would be part of the plant staff, they might have a "dotted-line" responsibility to central purchasing in regard to vendor selection, order quantities, lead times, etc.

In cases where the company has a central computer and only one MRP II software package and the central data processing group does all the Material Requirements Planning processing, purchasing would have the option to do vendor scheduling at the central location or the plant site. Since all plant requirements are run on the same software, it would be very easy to get the combined requirements for every item for every location on one Material Requirements Planning report. This would let buyers give each vendor a vendor schedule which showed the total requirements for each item, just as if there were only a single location. This would be far simpler for the vendor than receiving five different plans from five different plants. At the same time, the vendor schedule would break down the total weekly quantity by plant location and tell him how much to ship to each plant weekly.

Regardless of which approach is employed, it may be advantageous to generate one corporate vendor schedule in situations where there are common parts used by several plants. It would display the total requirements for that item, along with shipping and delivery information. In fact, some companies use a combination of approaches. On large-volume multiple-plant items, a central scheduling group handles those items. On parts that are unique to a plant and purchased at a vendor located close to the plant, a plant scheduling group handles those items. In cases where some parts are purchased overseas by someone located in an overseas buying office, those items can be scheduled from that location. MRP II can provide a great deal of flexibility in establishing "who does what and where." We'll have some more examples of organizational flexibility in the next chapter, on Special Situations.

Chapter 4
Special Situations

Up to now, we've discussed vendor scheduling only as it applies to somewhat routine production items. This chapter will cover special applications of this technique. First we'll address the topic of buying "tough" commodities (such as integrated circuits). Next, we'll cover some of the issues involved in small companies and in "process" and repetitive manufacturers. This chapter will also discuss using vendor scheduling in a distribution company as opposed to a manufacturing firm. We'll conclude with an overview of planning and scheduling Maintenance, Repair and Operating (MRO) supplies.

Buying Tough Commodities

Depending on business conditions, all commodities can become difficult to acquire from time to time. Lead times for integrated circuits, for example, can vary dramatically over a year's time, creating special problems. As the demand for the commodity increases, its lead time may lengthen dramatically. Individual items within the commodity, as well as the commodity as a whole, may go on allocation. Oliver Wight likened this phenomenon to a funnel (see Figure 4-1).

The vendor has a certain capacity, represented by the bottom of the funnel. The maximum rate at which the vendor can produce is shown by the rate of fluid flowing through the bottom. Obviously, if orders come in at a rate greater than the vendor's capacity, the level of orders in the backlog will increase and the vendor's lead time gets longer. At a certain level, represented by

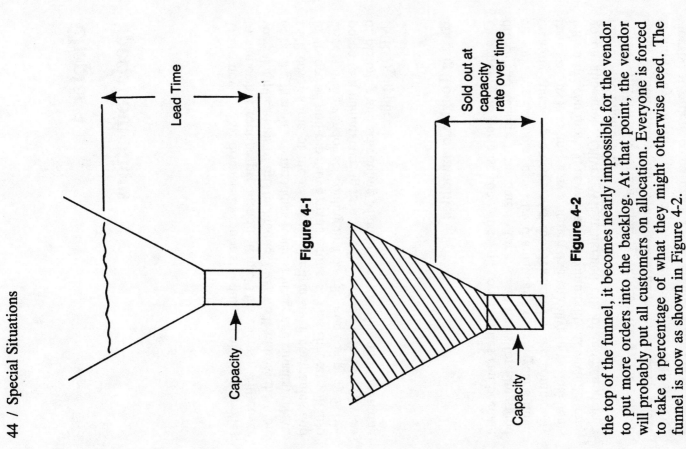

Figure 4-1

Figure 4-2

the top of the funnel, it becomes nearly impossible for the vendor to put more orders into the backlog. At that point, the vendor will probably put all customers on allocation. Everyone is forced to take a percentage of what they might otherwise need. The funnel is now as shown in Figure 4-2.

The allocation can be very serious for a company if it is less than its real needs. An excellent way to avoid this situation is to work out, before the allocation situation occurs, an agreement with the vendor to set aside a certain percentage of his capacity. Let's suppose that amounts to four hours a week of the capacity of a particular piece of equipment. If the vendor runs it for 24 hours a day, 7 days a week, the total output from that piece of equipment is 168 hours. Using the capacity planning information, the buyer learns he needs to contract for 2.4 percent of that capacity each week. That's represented by the thick line at the bottom of the funnel (see Figure 4-3).

Now it makes no difference if the vendor's quoted lead time goes from 6 weeks to 60. The buyer is still able to schedule 2.4 percent of the vendor's capacity on a weekly basis. Even if the vendor goes on allocation, the company still gets 2.4 percent of that equipment's capacity because of the contract the buyer has negotiated. That "tough" commodity is now much easier to manage. Based upon individual needs for the items the buyer has scheduled capacity for, he can always count on getting his four hours of capacity each day, each week, or each month from the vendor.

However, this approach to scheduling capacity and selecting

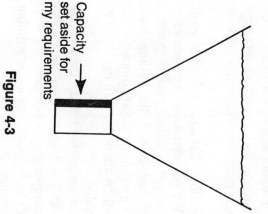

Capacity → set aside for my requirements

Figure 4-3

out of that capacity what is needed is not a panacea. It will take a lot of work, in some cases, to understand how the vendor schedules the item and how many work centers are involved at his manufacturing facility. If multiple work centers are involved at his facility, this approach may be difficult to negotiate with the vendor. But if a capacity reservation *can* be negotiated, then vendor scheduling will be much easier for those tough commodities.

Small Companies

It's often claimed that vendor scheduling is a good concept for large companies, but not for small ones. Buyers for smaller businesses may believe they have no "clout" with their vendors and that the system therefore won't work the same way for them. This belief implies that clout is all it takes to get vendor performance—that unless someone buys in high volumes, the vendor really isn't interested in his business. This is simply not true in most cases. If it were, the large companies would never run out of any parts and would always get first call on vendor capacity. Yet almost everyone has heard about large companies that have missed their monthly production goals due to lack of purchased parts.

It isn't always clout that counts; it's the quality of the schedule that matters. We've seen small companies with good vendor schedules able to get excellent vendor performance in all types of market conditions. In fact, the findings reported in Appendix B show that 80 percent of these companies surveyed purchased less than $30 million annually, with two companies spending only $4 million annually.

When vendors understand what the vendor schedule means, and how they can use it to maximize their planning to meet customer needs, company size becomes far less important. Even small companies have found vendor scheduling improves vendor delivery performance dramatically.

"Process" Companies

Companies in process industries, such as chemicals or paper, typically run on a continuous basis. Shutting down a glass furnace, for example, is very expensive. All raw materials required must be continuously available. Since they are always running, such plants tend to use very large quantities of basic raw materials quickly. It's quite common to bring in tank cars or trucks of chemicals weekly or even more frequently. Often, the storage facilities for these basic chemicals can't hold more than a few days' supply, so inventory turnover tends to be very high. Vendor scheduling fits well into this type of environment.

Most process plants have a daily production schedule, which becomes in effect the master production schedule in MRP II. They also have formulations or recipes (bills of material) for their products. Because of the need to maintain continuous production, process companies regularly verify the on-hand inventory of all raw materials. These elements, of course, are the key ingredients for Material Requirements Planning: a master schedule, bills of material, and the inventory status. By breaking the vendor schedule down into a daily schedule on purchased items, the purchasing department can schedule deliveries to arrive on the day needed. Here also, vendor scheduling handles the daily scheduling tasks and allows the buyer to spend his time on negotiations, alternate sourcings, etc.

One potential variable in certain process companies is the yield of the end product. Process variables or process problems may cause the yield to differ from day to day. In other words, it may take more raw materials than expected to produce the total batch weight desired. This is somewhat analogous to the scrap some manufacturers in nonprocess industries experience on raw materials. If the company can forecast scrap or yield variances, they can be expressed in the bill of material. If they can't be anticipated, the replanning feature of MRP will take these yield variables into consideration. If production takes more of a particular raw material than anticipated, the on-hand inventory will reflect this. MRP would then recalculate the need date based upon the lower inventory and advise the vendor scheduler accordingly. Therefore, the vendor schedule can reflect the true need date on each item bought, taking into account all the variables of the process.

Replanning is one of the strong features of MRP. It not only plans the first time, but replans based upon the current situation. Reorder points and other ordering systems don't have this replanning capability. The MRP-generated vendor schedule in a process company can be a natural to support a continuous process.

Repetitive Manufacturers

High-volume repetitive manufacturing is another natural for vendor scheduling. By definition, the same parts are being used over and over again—day in, day out. High-volume repetitive situations lend themselves readily to Just-in-Time scheduling, as we'll discuss in Chapter 8. In many repetitive environments, where the items required are fairly simple to manufacture, the vendor schedule can actually be used as the vendor's own production schedule.

As an example, suppose a company uses wood in its product and the only variable is the length of the piece. The company makes 1,000 end items per week and requires the wood pieces to be either 6″, 6½″, or 7″ in length, depending upon which version of the end item is scheduled for production. The vendor would set aside the capacity required to make 1,000 cuts on a table saw. The vendor schedule would be given directly to the operator of the table saw, and it would tell him how many of each length to cut each day or each week.

Since the purchased parts are repetitive, the vendor schedule tends to be much more stable in these cases. This makes vendor planning of capacity and raw materials much more efficient and should allow better pricing stability. If a company produces 20,000 chairs per week, and each chair takes one yard of fabric, the vendor knows he needs the yarn and capacity equal to 20,000 yards every week. The vendor is able, therefore, to do a better job of planning and to secure stable pricing and supply with his vendors. This further assures his customers of a constant product at a consistent price over time. Vendor scheduling is well suited to highly repetitive companies.

Distributors

Distributors are different from the companies discussed so far in this book. With few exceptions, they don't manufacture any of the items they sell. Typically, they purchase finished items from various manufacturers and resell them to retailers.

Distribution companies can develop vendor agreements for all the items they buy from a manufacturer, and then schedule in the items as they are needed. Sound familiar? That's what all buyers do, whether they're purchasing castings, fasteners, or finished items for resale, such as hammers or cosmetics, or whatever.

Let's look at the sources of demand on a distribution company's buyer using Distribution Resource Planning, part of an MRP II system. In this example (see Figure 4-4), there are three regional distribution centers (DCs) and one central distribution center. The central DC replenishes the regionals, which ship to customers. In addition, the central DC services customers in its area. Each regional DC would have a sales forecast and an on-hand inventory for every item and would also know what is in-transit from the central DC.

On the hammers it stocks, the Dallas DC has a forecast of 70 per week, 120 currently on hand in inventory, and 200 in transit from the distribution center due next week (period one). (See Figure 4-5.) Distribution Resource Planning would calculate when Dallas will need more hammers (planned orders).

Dallas will need to receive a shipment of 200 hammers in week 4 and another shipment of 200 hammers in week 7, to avoid going below the safety stock of 100. Given the two-week replenishment lead time, the central DC will need to ship to Dallas in weeks 2 and 5; hence the planned order releases of 200 in each of these weeks. These Dallas planned orders are input to the central DC's

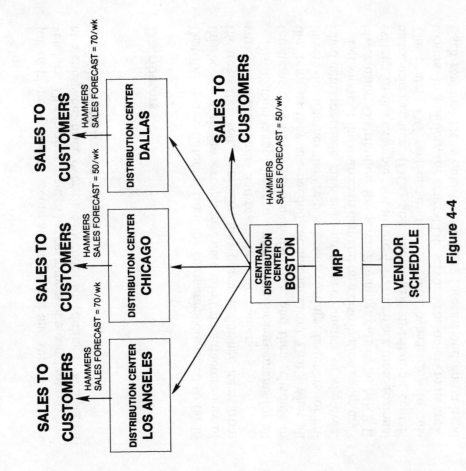

Figure 4-4

Material Requirements Planning system for the hammer, along with the planned orders from the other two DCs and the regional distribution center.

Note that Los Angeles orders in quantities of 200 and Chicago, in quantities of 100. DRP then calculates a schedule of the total requirements for hammers to be delivered from the manufacturer to the distribution center. (See Figure 4-6.)

The planned order information for hammer A at the central distribution center in Boston is consolidated via MRP onto the

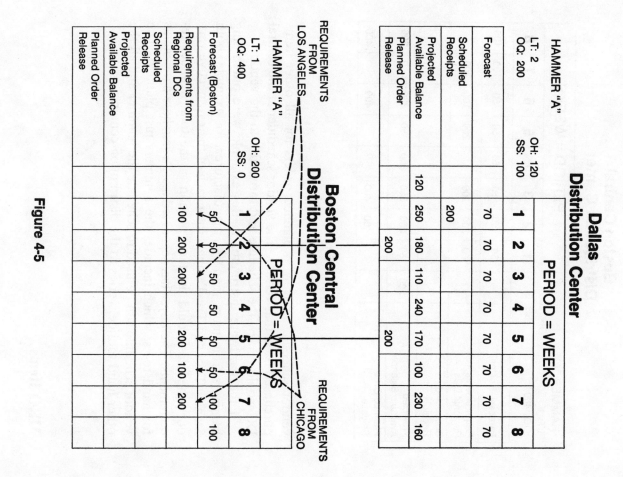

Figure 4-5

Boston Central
Distribution Center

HAMMER "A"
LT: 1   OH: 200
OQ: 400   SS: 0

	PERIOD = WEEKS							
	1	2	3	4	5	6	7	8
Forecast (Boston)	50	50	50	50	50	50	100	100
Requirements from Regional DCs	100	200	200		200	100	200	
Scheduled Receipts								
Projected Available Balance	200	50	200	350	300	50	300	0	300
Planned Order Release		400	400			400		400

Figure 4-6

vendor schedule along with planned orders for all other items purchased from that vendor. The vendor scheduler at the central DC would review the schedule and forward it to the vendor.

If the hardware distributor in this example were purchasing hammers from more than one manufacturer, for example, both Stanley Tool and Tru-Temper, then each of their respective vendor schedules would list their portion of the total hammer requirements. The buyer has negotiated master purchase agreements for hand tools, which includes the hammers just planned. The vendor schedule can be used to schedule the hammer and all the other hand tool deliveries to the distribution center.

MRO Items

The typical Maintenance, Repair and Operating (MRO) buyer is drowning in paperwork. Consider that if he buys 20,000 items an average of three times a year, that's 60,000 requisitions, 60,000 purchase orders, and 60,000 receiving reports. It's no wonder the MRO buyer has little time to do anything but shuffle paper. Because of this time constraint, the buyer typically finds it hard to do systems contracting or value analysis on the MRO items.

These items, however, can be handled and scheduled in much the same way as production items. To schedule any item on MRP, three things are needed: a master schedule on the end item, an inventory record on each item, and a bill of material that includes every item to schedule. Let's look at the bill of material.

First, every item must have an item number so the system can keep track of it. This may be a problem for some companies that do not currently have item numbers assigned to MRO items. Those companies would have to assign item numbers for all the MRO items that they want to schedule on MRP II.

The second requirement of the bill of material is the quantity of each item to be scheduled. For example, suppose that a piece of consumable tooling, such as a drill bit used in manufacturing an item, needs to be replaced. On average, the drill bit is replaced after producing ten parts, so the quantity per for that drill bit would be 1/10th. For every ten parts required, the MRP II system will require one drill bit.

The third requirement of the bill of material is a structure showing how the item is used. This structure is represented by Figure 4-7.

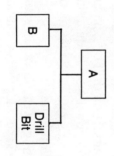

Figure 4-7

If the job demands 100 of part A, the system would plan a requirement for ten drill bits and 100 undrilled parts (B), then schedule the drilling work center to complete the drilling operation. Likewise, if the drilling operation requires cooling oil, that could be scheduled by making it a component of part A as well. See Figure 4-8.

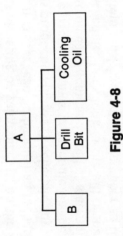

Figure 4-8

By including the cost of the consumable tooling or the operating supplies in the product costs, a company can get a more accurate total cost of producing a product. On the other hand, some companies may not want these expense items in the product cost. By setting the costs of the drill bit and cooling oil at zero, they can be scheduled using MRP and not affect the product cost.

An inventory record on the drill bit and cooling oil is required to determine the starting on-hand balance. If there are eight drill bits on hand and the MRP system requires ten, it would indicate at least two more must be acquired to meet the production schedule. The master schedule, the schedule of the end items to be built on a weekly or daily basis, would then drive the week-by-week drill bit requirements. These drill requirements would then be scheduled from the vendor on the vendor schedule. The buyer would negotiate a contract on drill bits, and the vendor scheduler would release the individual weekly quantities to the vendor. In this way, the operating supplies would be scheduled exactly the same as the production items.

Here's an interesting twist on organization. In one company we know, the vendor scheduler for consumable tooling—drill bits, saw blades, reamers, etc.—is a member of the industrial engineering department. In another company, the vendor scheduler for packaging material is in shipping. Good basic systems (knowing what's needed and when) and short, clear lines of communications (vendor scheduling) permit organizational flexibility, one aspect of which is being able to put functions "where the action is."

The maintenance items for the equipment in the factory can also be vendor scheduled. Most companies have a regular preventive maintenance schedule. This can become the "master schedule." Each piece of equipment is given a number, such as Press #1 (P1), Press #2 (P2), and so on. When the maintenance staff plans the preventive maintenance on an individual piece of equipment, they intend to replace certain items. These items are then structured into the bill of material as shown in Figure 4-9.

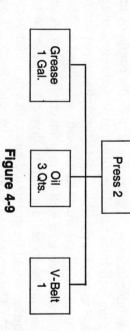

Figure 4-9

If the lead time on each of these items to be used is one week, and the maintenance on Press P2 is scheduled for the week of July 15th, MRP would schedule the items needed from the vendor, releasing the orders in the week of July 8th.

This approach can also be adapted to work for items that aren't replaced consistently. Suppose that when the company does preventive maintenance on a piece of equipment, it's not always necessary to replace the V-belt. By checking the maintenance records, it's possible to see it's necessary to replace it only 80 percent of the time. The company can put a .8 fractional quantity in the bill of material. MRP will then compensate for this and schedule in the correct quantity of the V-belts.

By inputting the annual preventive maintenance schedule for all the equipment in the factory into the master production schedule, preventive maintenance parts can be placed on a vendor schedule. Now that the buyer knows the annual requirements for oil, grease, V-belts, and so on, he can negotiate annual contracts on these items with releases as required. Like the production item buyer, the MRO buyer is spending his time contracting, *not* handling pieces of paper.

This technique can be extended to office supplies, hand tools, pipe fittings, ad infinitum. Here's an illustration. Most companies have a central stockroom that contains all the office supplies. Every item in the stockroom can be assigned an item number, which could, if desired, match the office supply vendor's catalog number for every item. An inventory record is created and a minimum inventory established for each item (such as one dozen ball-point pens). When someone needs a pen, it is issued from stock. When the inventory drops below the minimum (in this case, to 11), the MRP system schedules a replacement shipment from the vendor in an appropriate lot size. If the company inputs a forecast on each item based on either expected future usage or on historical usage, it's possible to get a time-phased requirements plan like that for all the other items being scheduled on MRP.

This idea works equally well for in-plant construction. A simple example would be to build a wall to divide a conference room. A work order would be generated and assigned a number, such as WO137. The maintenance manager would develop a "parts list" of the materials needed to complete the wall. This parts list would be input to the computer in the form of a bill of material. The end item number would be the same as the work order number. See Figure 4-10.

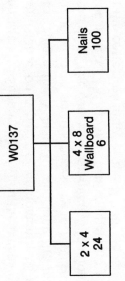

Figure 4-10

Purchasing has negotiated a "list-less" contract with the local lumber yard covering all purchases for the year (that is, the published *list* price on all the items, *less* an across-the-board discount on all purchases). The maintenance department determines they can do the job in six hours, and schedules the job for September 15. The lead time on the purchased items is two days. On September 13, the vendor schedule triggers the delivery of the various items required from the lumber yard. On September 15, the maintenance dispatch list would schedule the wall to be built. When the wall is completed, the work order is indicated as complete and the one-time bill of material is removed from the system. Again, the vendor schedule has been utilized to bring in the purchased parts on time.

Permanent tooling—both new tooling and preventive maintenance of existing tooling—can be scheduled in much the same way. By structuring a bill of activities (Figure 4-11), it's possible to schedule all the activities necessary to have the new tool on the date required. When the tooling request is completed on 6/1, the operation is reported as complete. The MRP system then schedules the design engineering department to complete the design, a draftsman to complete the drawing specification, and lastly, the actual building of the tool.

MRP II is fundamentally a network scheduling system. Project activities of a one-time nature, like designing and building a tool, typically scheduled by PERT (Project Evaluation and Review Technique), CPM (Critical Path Method), or other scheduling systems, can be scheduled via MRP II. A planning bill of material, or bill of activities as in Figure 4-11, is used instead of the PERT or CPM chart. Once established, this planning bill of material or bill of activities is entered into the computer just like a standard bill of material. Then, as each step is completed, the MRP system schedules the next operation in time to meet the end completion

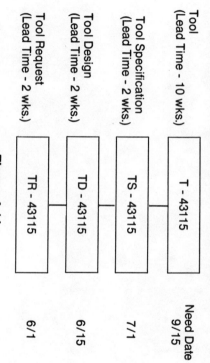

	Need Date
Tool (Lead Time - 10 wks.)	T - 43115 9/15
Tool Specification (Lead Time - 2 wks.)	TS - 43115 7/1
Tool Design (Lead Time - 2 wks.)	TD - 43115 6/15
Tool Request (Lead Time - 2 wks.)	TR - 43115 6/1

Figure 4-11

date of the project. Companies have even erected buildings using MRP II scheduling techniques. MRP II has the capabilities to schedule *all of the resources* needed in a company and shouldn't be seen as just *manufacturing* resource planning.

MRP II/vendor scheduling works as well for the distributor as the manufacturer, in large companies and small, process control, repetitive, or one-of-a-kind manufacturing companies. It represents a universal solution to a universal problem in purchasing: too little time to do a professional buying job. Vendor scheduling is limited only by the user's imagination and perception of what it can do.

Chapter 5

MRP II Implementation Part I—Company-Wide

The process of implementing vendor scheduling in purchasing needs to be integrated with the overall task of implementing MRP II throughout the company. In this chapter, we'll provide an overview of the company-wide implementation process. Chapter 6 will concentrate on the specifics of implementing vendor scheduling. In this way, purchasing people can gain an understanding of "the big picture," as well as their department's role in the implementation process.[1]

Catch-22

There's a "Catch-22" involved in implementing MRP II successfully. It goes like this:

It's a whole lot of work. Implementing MRP II properly requires a great deal of time and effort on the parts of many people throughout the company. Many things must be done: Data must be made more accurate, much education must take place, new software must be acquired and installed, new policies and procedures must be developed and made operational, and on and on.

It's a do-it-yourself project. Successful implementations are done internally. Virtually all of the work involved must be

[1] For more detailed information on the implementation process, consult *MRP II: Making It Happen—The Implementers' Guide to Success with Manufacturing Resource Planning* by Thomas F. Wallace, published by Oliver Wight Limited Publications, Inc., Essex Junction, VT, 1985.

done by the company's own people. The responsibility can't be turned over to outsiders such as consultants or software vendors. That's been tried repeatedly and hasn't been shown to work well at all. Where implementation responsibility is decoupled from operational responsibility, who can legitimately be accountable for results? If results aren't forthcoming, the implementers can claim the users aren't operating it properly, while the users can say that it wasn't implemented correctly. Almost without exception, the companies who have become Class A users (see Appendix C for an explanation of Class A, B, C, D) have been the ones where the users themselves implemented MRP II.

It's not the number one priority in the company. The first priority is to make shipments, meet the payroll, keep the equipment running . . . to run the business. All other activities must be subordinate. Implementing MRP II can't be number one, but it does need to be pegged as a very high number two priority.

This Catch-22 is one of the reasons why many companies that implement MRP II never get beyond Class C. Other reasons include:

It's people-intensive. MRP II is commonly misperceived as a computer system. Not so. It's a *people* system made possible by the computer.

Many early attempts at implementation focused on the computer and the software. They neglected the people. Ollie Wight said it well: "If you consider MRP II as a computer system to order parts, what you'll probably wind up with is a computer system to order parts. On the other hand, if you look upon MRP II as a set of tools with which to run the business far more effectively, and if you implement it correctly, that's exactly what you'll get."

Well, who runs the business? People do. People like buyers, foremen, engineers, marketeers, planners—and their managers, and their managers' managers, up to and including the general manager.

It involves virtually every department within the company. It's not enough for just manufacturing or purchasing or distribution to be "on board." Virtually all departments in the company must be deeply involved in implementing MRP II; purchasing, marketing, engineering, quality, manufacturing, finance, personnel, purchasing, and so on.

It requires people to do their jobs differently. Companies implementing MRP II must undergo massive behavior change to be successful. MRP II requires a "new set of values." Many things must be done differently, and this kind of transformation is never easy to achieve.

Experienced users say implementing MRP II is far more difficult than building a new plant, introducing a new product, or entering a whole new market. Breaking through the Catch-22, overcoming the people problems, making it happen—these are the challenges. That's the bad news.

The good news is there's a way to meet these challenges. There's no mystery involved. Implementing MRP II successfully can be almost a sure thing—*if it's done right.* Yes, it is a lot of work. But it's virtually no risk—*if you do it right.* MRP II has never failed to work, not once, when correctly implemented. It *will* work and the company will realize enormous benefits.

The Proven Path

Back in the late 1960s and early 1970s, there was no clearly defined method for implementing MRP II. Out of that era of trial-and-error experimentation, there gradually developed a body of knowledge about how to implement. Today, that knowledge has been concentrated into a set of implementation steps called the "Proven Path." If followed faithfully, this Proven Path enables companies to break through the Catch-22. It virtually guarantees a successful implementation.

The bar chart in Figure 5-1 shows a graphic representation of the eleven steps of the Proven Path. Each step is summarized briefly below.

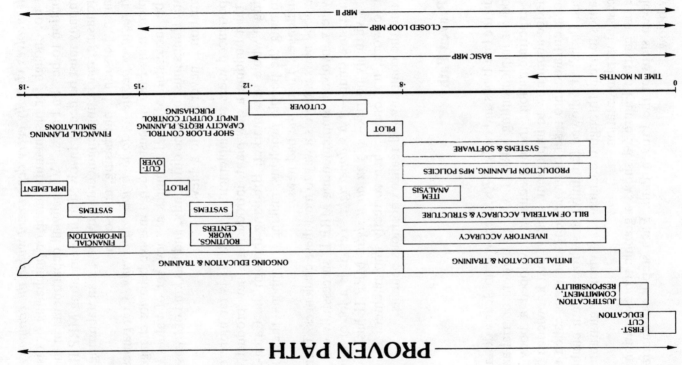

Figure 5-1

Step #1. *First-Cut Education.* A handful of executives and key operating managers from within the company must learn about MRP II before they can do a proper job of step #2 (Cost Justification and Commitment). They should attend "outside" classes taught by qualified MRP II professionals. In these classes they'll be with their peers from other companies. In this environment, they can see that their companies are not unique and they all share common problems that can be resolved by using MRP II. Since first-cut education precedes the final decision to implement, attendees should be limited to key people who will have accountability for both costs and benefits.

Step #2. *Cost Justification and Commitment.* After the key people within the company have returned from outside classes, they should begin to calculate their costs and benefits relative to MRP II. This cost justification process is necessary to establish MRP II as a high priority in the company. If the benefits, both tangible and intangible, don't justify the costs involved, the company should stop there and not proceed with MRP II. Without a wholehearted commitment from the beginning, the implementation has little chance for success.

To help get a clear focus on implementation issues, we talk about the ABC's of MRP II. The computer is the "C" item, the hardware and the software. While they're essential, they're of lesser significance than the other elements. The "B" item is the data, such as inventory records, bills of material, routings, etc. These items are more significant and require more of the company's overall attention and managerial emphasis. The "A" item is the people. It's the key element in making MRP II work. If this aspect of the implementation project is managed properly, then the people will understand the objectives and how to get there.

These categories are also useful in discussing the typical costs involved in MRP II systems.

C—The "computer" costs include any new hardware necessary, plus purchased (or leased) software for MRP II. Also, funds should be allocated for systems analysts and programmers. Their job is to install and debug the purchased software, make necessary modifications and enhancements, probably write some new software internally, interface the purchased software with existing systems, assist in user training, develop documentation, and provide system maintenance. Other costs include those for software maintenance contracts, forms, supplies, etc.

B—The costs involved in getting and maintaining accurate data may include new fences, gates, scales, shelves, bins, lift trucks and other new equipment to ensure inventory record accuracy. The plant may need to be laid out differently to create and/or consolidate stockrooms, and additional manpower, such as cycle counters, might also be needed in the stockroom area. There probably will be other costs to correct routings, and to create complete, accurate, and properly structured bills of material. Item data, sales forecasts, work center data, and other information may also need attention. Typically, these are not areas of major expense, and they don't consume huge amounts of time.

A—The "people" costs involved in implementation include salaries for full-time people on the project team, outside education for key people (including travel and lodging), and the cost of in-house education programs for the remainder of the company. Also, it's vital to acquire the services of an experienced MRP II consultant to provide professional guidance.

The benefits that can be expected usually fall into these general categories:

1. *Increased sales* as a result of improved customer service and the ability to ship faster and more dependably than the competition.

2. *Increased direct labor productivity* due to fewer shortages, less expediting, few emergency changeovers, reduced overtime, and so forth.

3. *Reduced purchase costs* because MRP II lets purchasing give vendors valid schedules and better forward visibility, and because vendor scheduling gives buyers the time they need for sourcing, negotiation, contracting, value analysis, cost reduction, etc. (In many companies, purchase cost reductions are the largest single benefit derived from MRP II.)

4. *Reduced inventories* as a result of valid schedules and matched sets of components.

5. *Reduced obsolescence* because of an enhanced ability to manage engineering changes.

6. *Reduced quality costs,* due to less scrap and rework, and lower warranty costs.

7. *Reduced premium freight* both inbound and outbound.

8. *Elimination of the annual physical inventory,* which does away with the costs of taking the inventory itself, and also the attendant disruption to production.

9. *Increased productivity of the indirect work force,* by reducing the need for expediting, and improving the quality of work life for all levels of employees.

The participants in the justification process should be those executives and managers who'll be held accountable for achieving the projected benefits within the framework of the identified costs.

This process should be participative in nature. Top management, as well as operating management, needs to be involved. This is far better than the more "traditional" approach, where the operating managers put together the cost justification and then attempt to "sell" the project to their bosses. If top management has been to first-cut education, there should be no need for them to "be sold." Rather, they and their key managers should be "selling themselves" on specifically how MRP II will benefit their company and what it'll cost to get to Class A.

Be fiscally conservative. When in doubt, estimate the costs to the high side of their probable range and the benefits, low. Don't promise more than you can deliver.

A Sample Cost Justification

To illustrate the process, let's create a hypothetical company with the following characteristics:

Annual Sales: $80 million
Employees: 750
Number of Plants: 1
Manufacturing Process: Fabrication and assembly
Product: A complex assembled product, make-to-order, with many options (electronics, machinery, etc.)
Pretax Net Profit: 8 percent of sales
Annual Direct Labor Cost: $8 million
Annual Purchase Volume (production materials): $24 million
Current Inventories: $18 million

Costs are divided into "one-time" (acquisition) costs and "recurring" (annual operating) costs . . . and are in our three categories: C-Computer, B-Data, A-People. See Figure 5-2.

Figure 5-2 Sample Company Cost Justification

COSTS C-Computer	One-time	Recurring	Comments
Hardware	$ 60,000	$36,000	Company T already has a computer, but will need to add some new hardware to it. Some of the new hardware will be purchased, and some will be leased at $3,000 per month.
Software	200,000	—	The most expensive software package being considered costs $200,000. They plan to maintain the software themselves, rather than buy the software vendor's maintenance service.
Systems and Programming	200,000	35,000	Data processing people costs to install the software, modify it to fit the business, interface it to existing systems, enhance it, maintain it, and to do documentation, training, etc.

Figure 5-2 Continued

B-Data	One-time	Recurring	Comments
Inventory Record Accuracy	235,000	30,000	Includes new equipment and one full-time cycle counter.
Bill of Material Accuracy and Structure	120,000	—	Bills will need to be restructured into the modular format. Experienced engineers will be required for this step.
Routing Accuracy	25,000	—	Routings are fairly accurate now, but will need to be reviewed.

A-People	One-time	Recurring	Comments
Project Team	$ 160,000	—	One full-time project leader and one assistant, for eighteen months.
Outside Education	100,000	10,000	Includes travel.
Inside Education	80,000	20,000	Includes costs for video, overtime costs, plus vendor education.
Professional Guidance	25,000	2,000	One-day visits, every four to eight weeks, by an experienced MRP II professional.
Total Costs	$1,205,000	$133,000	

BENEFITS Function	Current	% Improvement	Annual Benefits	Comments
Sales	$80,000,000	5% at 8%	$320,000	Sales and marketing is projecting a 5% sales gain due to improved customer service. The company's net profit has been running at 8% of sales.
Direct Labor Productivity	8,000,000	5%	400,000	
Purchase Cost Reduction	24,000,000	2.5%	600,000	

Figure 5-2 Continued

BENEFITS Function	Current	% Improvement	Annual Benefits	Comments
Inventory Reduction	18,000,000	20% at 15%	540,000	The inventory is projected to decrease by 20%. A carrying cost of 15% was used.
Obsolescence	250,000	20%	50,000	
Warranty Cost Reduction	400,000	25%	100,000	
Premium Freight	100,000	50%	50,000	
Annual Physical Inventory	50,000	100%	50,000	
Gross Annual Benefits			$2,370,000	
Subtracting: Recurring Costs			−133,000	
Net Annual Benefits			$2,237,000	

	Divided by 12
Cost of a One-Month Delay	$186,416
Payback Period (one-time costs/(net annual benefits/12))	6.5 Months, Following Full Implementation
Return on Investment (net annual benefits/one-time costs)	185%

MRP II appears to be very attractive for this company, showing an excellent return on investment of 164 percent. Please note that the largest single financial benefit is purchase cost reduction.

Commitment

There's one final acid test for implementation readiness: Is the company prepared to keep MRP II as a very high priority effort for the next several years? If the answer is no, don't go ahead.

If the answer is yes, the people who developed the numbers in the cost justification need to *commit* to them. A good way to do this is through a written project charter, a document that affirms everyone's commitment to achieving the benefits planned within the costs and time frame stated. This written charter not only stresses the importance of the project, but serves as a rallying point during the project ahead.

Step #3. User-Controlled Project Team. As we mentioned earlier, the people who implement MRP II must be those who will later be held accountable for operating it. The project team is responsible for implementing MRP II at the *operational* level in the company. It consists of relatively few *full-time* members, such as the project leader and his assistants and often one or more data processing people. Most of the members are *part-time*. They're the department heads—the operating managers of the business.

The project team meets once or twice a week for about an hour. It's responsible for:

- Establishing the MRP II project schedule.
- Reporting actual performance against the schedule.
- Identifying problems and obstacles to successful implementation.
- Activating ad hoc groups, called "spin-off" task forces, to solve these problems.
- Making decisions regarding priorities, resource allocation, etc.
- Making recommendations to the "executive steering committee" (discussed in Step #5).
- Doing whatever else is required to make the implementation a success at the operational level.

Since the purchasing department will become one of the major users of the system, the purchasing manager plays a key role on the project team. He'll be a member of the team, often with responsibilities for "spin-off task forces" within his area of expertise, such as acquiring the software for vendor scheduling or developing the vendor education program.

Step #4. *Full-Time Project Leader.* At least one key person from within the company should be freed from all other responsibilities to manage the implementation effort. Every company needs at least one person for whom MRP II is the first priority. Part-time project leaders almost invariably have to give preference to operational responsibilities. This will delay the project and decrease its chances for success.

Typically, the project leader will have the following responsibilities:

- Chairing the MRP II project team.

- Acting as a member of the executive steering committee.

- Overseeing the educational process—both inside and outside.

- Coordinating the preparation of the project schedule and obtaining concurrence and commitment from everyone involved.

- Updating the project schedule weekly and highlighting the jobs behind schedule.

- Counseling those behind schedule and helping them get back on schedule.

- Reporting serious delays to the executive steering committee, and making recommendations on their resolution.

- Rescheduling the project as necessary under the direction of the executive steering committee.

- Working closely with the outside consultant and keeping him advised of progress and problems.

- Removing obstacles and supporting the people doing the work, that is, the operational managers.

The project leader should be chosen from the ranks of the operating managers, the department heads. We've seen purchasing managers make excellent MRP II project leaders.

We recommend against hiring the project leader from outside the company, nor do we feel it's a good idea to move a data processing person into the project leader's job. What's required is a "heavyweight," a person with a solid operational background, a good track record, and in-depth knowledge of the company's products, processes, and people.

Step #5. *Executive Steering Committee.* Top management has overall responsibility for success with MRP II. The general manager and his staff lead the implementation process and carry out their responsibility via this steering committee, which meets about twice per month for about an hour.

The steering committee's role is to review delays in the project schedule and make decisions on rescheduling and reallocating resources. Its members may also have to address other issues, such as unforeseen obstacles, problem individuals in key positions, and difficulties with the software vendor.

Step #6. *Professional Guidance.* Implementing an MRP II system is not an extension of past experience; it's a whole new way of running the company. Companies need periodic access to someone who has been deeply involved in one or more Class A implementations. This person will serve as a catalyst, a sounding board, an adviser, and a "conscience" to top management. His job is to force the project team to face the tough issues and focus on the right priorities.

Consultants should *not* write procedures, draw flow charts, write job descriptions, develop computer program specifications and so on. These jobs belong to people within the company. Consultants should visit the company only about one or two days every month or two. Too much consulting takes initiative and responsibility away from the project team and deprives the company of a sense of "ownership" of their own system.

Step #7. *Education of the Critical Mass.* Education for MRP II has two critically important objectives. The first is *fact transfer,* which refers to the transmission of information on the whats, whys, and hows. While it's essential, it's not nearly enough. The second objective of education for MRP II, far more important and far more difficult than the mere transfer of facts, is *behavior change.* It has some profound implications.

The successful implementation of Manufacturing Resource Planning within a company results in being able to run the business far better than before. Running the business better than before implies, of course, running it differently. On a macro level, therefore, implementing MRP II means changing the way the business is run. On a micro basis this translates to hundreds, perhaps thousands of people willingly and enthusiastically changing the way they do their jobs.

It's an awesome task. Change, for most people, doesn't come easy. How many of us have ever heard (or perhaps asked) the question: "Why do we need to do it differently? We've been doing it the same way for the last twelve years and we're getting along OK"?

A key element in the Proven Path, perhaps the most important of all, is doing education effectively. Doing education effectively is synonymous with managing the process of change. Behavior change therefore is a process, via which people come to believe in this new set of tools and "acquire ownership" of it. MRP II then becomes "the way we're going to run the business."

Executing the process of behavior change—education for MRP II—is a management issue, not a technical one. The results of this process are groups of people who believe in this new way to run the business and who are prepared to change the way they do their jobs to make it happen.

The Criteria for Change

There are eight criteria for developing a program to facilitate behavior change:

1. *Active top management leadership and participation in the education process.* These are the most important people of all, and within this group, the general manager is the most important person. Failure to educate top management, particularly the general manager, is probably the single most significant cause of companies not succeeding with MRP II. Why? For many reasons, one being the law of organizational gravity. Change must cascade down the organization chart; it doesn't flow uphill.

2. *Line accountability for education.* People are the "A" item, and education is the key to the people. To exclude operating managers from the process of educating their own people seriously weakens the degree to which they can be held accountable for the success of MRP II within their departments.

3. *Total immersion for key people.* The operating managers need to go through the change process themselves before they can lead others through it. These people, who are experts in running their parts of the business, need to become experts on how MRP II will operate within the company.

4. *Total coverage throughout the company.* Education must be very widespread throughout the company because almost everyone will be involved with MRP II in one way or another—either directly or indirectly. The question to ask here is not "whom to educate" but rather "whom to exclude."

5. *Continuing reinforcement.* Once is not enough. To really learn the important things, people usually need to hear them more than once.

6. *Instructor credibility.* Education for MRP II comes in two formats—outside and inside. Both are necessary. It's essential that some key people go to live outside classes, to start to become the company's "experts" on MRP II. It's essential that the instructors of these classes already be experts, that they've been deeply involved in successful implementations and hence can speak from first-hand experience. If not, credibility will suffer and behavior change for the key people may never get started.

Since it's obviously not practical to send everyone to outside classes, education in-plant is also necessary. The instructors of these classes must not only be knowledgeable on MRP II; they must be "experts" on the company—its products, its processes, its people, its customers, its vendors, etc. If not, credibility will suffer and behavior change for the critical mass may never happen. Outsiders can't be experts on the company, no matter how much they may know about MRP II. The experts on the company are, of course, the operating managers.

7. *Peer confirmation.* Education for MRP II should not be of the individual, programmed-instruction variety. Reading books

just won't get the behavior change job done. People need to have the opportunity to ask questions and, more important, be able to hear their co-workers ask questions and receive satisfactory answers. This can be very reassuring. It's far easier for an individual to buy in, if the group is buying in.

8. *Enthusiasm.* Remember the Catch-22 of Manufacturing Resource Planning? It's a lot of work; we have to do it ourselves; it's not the number one priority. Widespread enthusiasm is one of the key elements needed to break through the Catch-22.

Enthusiasm comes about when people begin mentally to match up their problems (late shipments, massive expediting, excessive overtime, parts shortages, finger pointing, funny numbers, and on and on) with MRP II as the solution. The kind of enthusiasm we're talking about here doesn't necessarily mean the flag-waving, rah-rah variety. More important is a solid conviction that MRP II makes sense, is valid, and, if implemented properly, can help solve many of the nagging problems which have been around for years. Ollie Wight had a good description of enthusiasm in this context; he called it "a sense of mission."

The Change Process

Thus far we've looked at the objectives of the MRP II education program, the most important by far being behavior change, and also the necessary criteria for such a program. Now let's look at the process itself, a process which will meet the above criteria and enable behavior change to happen.

The future team of experts has already been identified—the department heads, the operating managers of the business. Let's now discuss how the operating management group within a company becomes a team of experts to facilitate and manage the change process. Very simply, this is done by having these people themselves go through the process of change. The following steps are involved:

1. Outside classes. It's essential for this future team of experts to get away from the office for an in-depth educational experience on MRP II. (See criterion #3—total immersion for key people.)

Such a class should not be "company-specific" or even "industry-specific." It's important that a variety of companies and industries be represented in the class. Then the future team of experts is much better able to work through the issue of uniqueness. They can learn that "We're not unique; we're not different; MRP II will work for us." Similarly, in such a class, there should be a variety of job functions represented such as production superintendents, purchasing managers, engineers, marketeers, accountants, and materials people. (See criterion #7—peer confirmation.)

Of course, these outside classes must be taught by MRP II professionals, people who have a solid track record of participating in successful Class A implementations of MRP II. These instructors need to be able to communicate not only the principles, techniques, and mechanics of MRP II, they must also be able to speak to results, the benefits which companies have realized from MRP II. (See criterion #6—instructor credibility.)

Here's some good news. Virtually all members of the future team of experts have already been to outside classes, as a part of First-Cut Education. In addition, a number of them will need to attend one or several specialty classes, which allow for more detailed and focused learning on specific topics. We'll discuss specifics for purchasing in Chapter 6.

2. A series of business meetings. Next on the agenda for these managers is a series of business meetings (called by some the "Teacher's Course"). The objectives here are to continue and to enhance the change process begun in the outside classes and to equip these operating managers with the tools to reach the critical mass.

Doing this properly requires a substantial amount of time, about 80 hours spread over several months. Not nearly as much time would be required here if the only objective were fact transfer. However, since the main objective is behavior change, a substantial commitment of time is necessary. (See criteria #3—total immersion for key people, and #5—continuing reinforcement.)

The agenda for these business meetings needs to be provided by the educational materials themselves. A variety of media are possible candidates. Today, however, companies serious about MRP II almost unvariably use professionally developed video taped courses, supplemented by printed material.

A key aspect of these business meetings is that approximately two-thirds of the time should be devoted to discussion. During these sessions, the educational materials (video, etc.) do the formal teaching; they communicate the principles, concepts, tools, and techniques of Manufacturing Resource Planning. However, the majority of the time in each session should be devoted to discussing application. This is where the operating managers determine how to apply these principles, concepts, tools, and techniques to manage their departments and hence how MRP II will be used to run the business.

It's essential that people be encouraged to ask the hard questions, to be skeptical in a constructive way. This process is what we call "bulletproofing" MRP II. People need to have opportunities to "take potshots" at MRP II, to try to shoot holes in it. Giving people answers which make sense helps to bulletproof MRP II. Making necessary changes to how the system will be used is further bulletproofing. Bulletproofing isn't instantaneous; it's not like turning on a light bulb. It's a gradual process, the result of responding to people's questions and being sensitive to their concerns.

People need to:

• understand it,
• think about it,
• talk to each other about it,
• ask questions about it and get answers,
• hear their peers ask questions about it and get answers,
• see how it will help them and help the company,

before they'll willingly and enthusiastically proceed to change the way they do their jobs.

Reaching the Critical Mass

Once the team of experts is created, the next step is for them to reach the critical mass. This is that majority of people within the company who are knowledgeable and enthusiastic about MRP II and who see the need and benefits from changing the way they do their jobs.

How is this accomplished? Very simply, by a series of business meetings. These are meetings conducted by the members of the team of experts (see criterion #6—instructor credibility) for all of the people within their respective departments (see criteria #2—line accountability for education—and #4—total coverage throughout the company).

How does one know if this change process is working? What's the test to apply as the sessions proceed? Here also, the test is enthusiasm (see criterion #8). If enthusiasm, teamwork, a sense of mission, and a sense of ownership are not visibly increasing during this process, then stop the process and fix it. Ask: What's missing? What's not being done properly? Which of the eight criteria are being violated? Is bulletproofing working, or are people not getting answers? (That means holes in MRP II, and not many people want to get onboard a leaky boat.)

When it's done properly, enthusiasm does develop. When it's done properly, the results are a critical mass of people who understand Manufacturing Resource Planning, who "own" it, and who are prepared to do their jobs differently to make it succeed.

Step #8. *Pilot Approach to MPS/MRP.* This step is designed to prove master production scheduling and material requirements planning are working satisfactorily on a "pilot" product line or group of items before cutting over all products and items. It demonstrates whether the software is working properly, plus also tests the user's understanding of the information the system is providing.

There are actually three types of pilots involved: the computer pilot, the conference room pilot, and the live pilot. The *computer pilot* is simply a very thorough check of the software: testing and debugging the programs on the computer using "dummy" items and data. Volume testing should also be done here. The *conference room pilot* is an education and training tool to help users learn more about the software and how to manage their part of the business with it. This part of the pilot can also help establish procedures and identify areas that may require policy direction. The *live pilot* is the point when the company starts running the pilot items on MPS/MRP and stops running them on the old system. Until the users are willing to state they can run their part of the business with these new tools, the other product lines should not be cut over onto the new system.

Companies should plan to run the live pilot for about a month, or longer if manufacturing cycles are long and speeds are slow. At this point, the rest of the items can be cutover onto MPS/MRP *provided that the pilot is working properly.* If not, fix what's wrong before cutting over.

Step #9. *Close the Loop.* At this stage in the implementation, the company begins tying the execution systems, such as vendor scheduling and shop floor control, into the planning systems. Like MPS/MRP, vendor scheduling and shop floor control should be tested by piloting before cutover.

At the beginning of closing the loop, the company is still in the traditional purchasing mode (with hard-copy purchase orders, requisitions, etc.). We'll discuss the details of implementing vendor scheduling in Chapter 6.

Step #10. *Finance and Simulation.* This step integrates the company's operating systems with its financial systems. The new financial systems should be run in parallel with the old ones, and their outputs compared. Most companies find they can discontinue running the old system after a few months of parallel operation. Step #10 also involves turning on MRP II's "what-if" capabilities, so management can use the system as a model to test alternative courses of action.

Step #11. *Dedication to Continuing Improvement.* Once a company reaches Class A status, it has to continue working hard to stay at that level of excellence. After it has reached that goal, it can begin to use the system as the "launch pad" for further improvements using new technologies such as Just-in-Time, CAD/CAM, Statistical Process Control, etc. For the purchasing department, this dedication means building closer, more honest relations with vendors than were ever possible before, working together on quality, implementing Just-in-Time. More on this in Chapter 9.

Chapter 6

MRP II Implementation Part II— Purchasing

In Chapter 5, we discussed how to implement a Class A MRP II system throughout the company using the *Proven Path*. This chapter will focus on implementing MRP II, including vendor scheduling in purchasing. Included in this chapter is a timetable to help purchasing people keep their implementation project in phase with the rest of the company.

There are many similarities between implementing MRP II in the company and in purchasing. Both begin with education, and both require effective project management. Both should follow a project plan and employ a pilot approach. Both require education of the "critical mass," and for purchasing this includes the vendors. Both require performance measurement criteria and a dedication to continuing improvement.

Education

The "whys" of education are spelled out in Chapter 5. Here, let's just reiterate that without the proper education, MRP II in purchasing will not be nearly as successful as it could. Both outside and inside education are necessary for purchasing if MRP II is to generate its true benefits.

As we said earlier, in most companies, purchase cost reduction represents the largest single payback from MRP II. Therefore, the purchasing manager must be a key part of the overall implementation effort. He needs to attend, as part of first-cut education, an in-depth class on MRP II (example: "MRP II: Manufacturing Resource Planning—The Five Day Class" by Oliver

Wight Education Associates or equivalent). With this background, he can participate fully in the cost justification process and should be able to make an informed commitment to the successful implementation of MRP II in purchasing.

Other key purchasing personnel, particularly in a larger company, may need to attend an in-depth class on MRP II. This should happen early in the life of the project, shortly after the decision to implement. These are people who, along with the purchasing manager, will be deeply involved in implementing MRP II in purchasing, perhaps an assistant purchasing manager and/or one or several senior buyers.

In addition, the purchasing manager and perhaps other key people will require more specific education on how to design, implement, and operate an MRP system in purchasing (example: "MRP II for Purchasing" by Oliver Wight Education Associates or equivalent). Also, the person selected to be the supervisor of the vendor scheduling group should also attend both of these kinds of classes.

These two education experiences enable the attendees to develop a complete and valid implementation plan for MRP II in purchasing and to assign responsibilities for the tasks in that plan. This timing gives them an opportunity to design the vendor schedule, the measurement reports, and the other tools prior to beginning inside education for the rest of the department. Having these in place in advance will strengthen the impact of the inside education.

As shown in Figure 6-1, inside video-based education should begin in month 3[1] and continue through month 8. The purchasing manager, as a member of the project team, would take part in the "teacher's course" during months 3 and 4. The "teacher's course" is that series of business meetings which we discussed in Chapter 5.

Between months 5 and 8, the entire purchasing department receives its inside education, with the purchasing manager acting

[1] Throughout this chapter, we'll make references to "month 3," "month 5" etc. These are not intended to be hard and fast times, but rather to represent approximately when various activities should begin and end.

PROVEN PATH

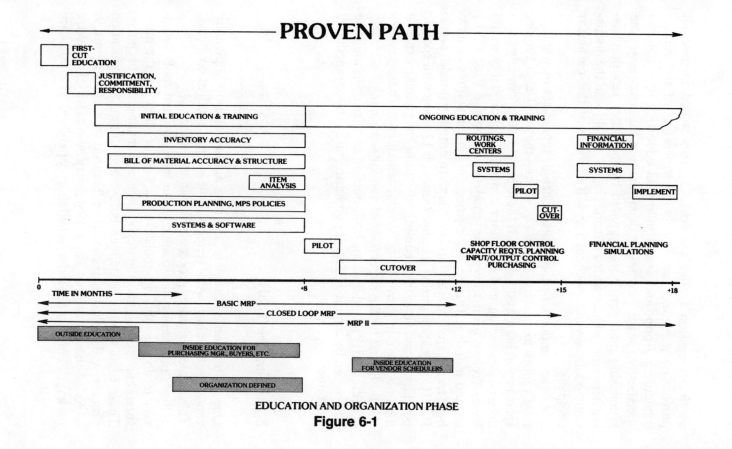

EDUCATION AND ORGANIZATION PHASE

Figure 6-1

as the discussion leader ("teacher"). This would include all purchasing personnel, as well as the supervisor of the vendor scheduling group, and would follow an education plan tailored specifically for the purchasing department in that company. The purchasing manager, possibly aided by the other key purchasing personnel who attended outside classes, would lead the discussions on how vendor scheduling will be done at this particular company.

As the vendor schedulers are selected, regardless of whether they report to purchasing or elsewhere, they will also require specific purchasing education. If these people were formerly planners in production and inventory control, they probably would have already been through internal education for P & IC by around month 8. If the vendor schedulers are new hires or have been transferred from an unrelated department, they should receive P & IC education during months 9 through 12 along with specific purchasing and vendor scheduling education and training explaining how the company will do vendor scheduling. These sessions should be led by the supervisor of vendor scheduling.

Initial MRP II education, both outside and inside, should be completed by month 12 for all purchasing and vendor scheduling personnel.

Specifying the Tools

Once education is complete, the next major step is to implement vendor scheduling with vendors who supply production items. This implementation process is shown in Figure 6-2.

First, purchasing has to specify the informational tools necessary to do the job. The tools are the vendor schedule, the measurement reports, and the negotiation and management reports. These tools should be defined before and during the education process, and their design should be finalized by around month 9.

As of this writing, in early 1986, very few MRP II software packages contain a vendor scheduling capability. The odds are

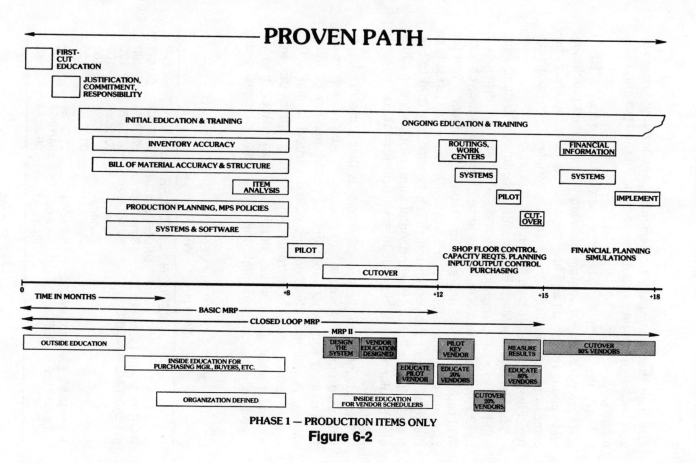

PROVEN PATH

FIRST-CUT EDUCATION

JUSTIFICATION, COMMITMENT, RESPONSIBILITY

| INITIAL EDUCATION & TRAINING | ONGOING EDUCATION & TRAINING |

INVENTORY ACCURACY

ROUTINGS, WORK CENTERS

FINANCIAL INFORMATION

BILL OF MATERIAL ACCURACY & STRUCTURE

SYSTEMS

SYSTEMS

ITEM ANALYSIS

PILOT

IMPLEMENT

PRODUCTION PLANNING, MPS POLICIES

CUT-OVER

SYSTEMS & SOFTWARE

PILOT

SHOP FLOOR CONTROL
CAPACITY REQTS. PLANNING
INPUT/OUTPUT CONTROL
PURCHASING

FINANCIAL PLANNING
SIMULATIONS

CUTOVER

| 0 | | +8 | | +12 | | +15 | | +18 |

TIME IN MONTHS

BASIC MRP

CLOSED LOOP MRP

MRP II

OUTSIDE EDUCATION

DESIGN THE SYSTEM

VENDOR EDUCATION DESIGNED

PILOT KEY VENDOR

MEASURE RESULTS

CUTOVER 80% VENDORS

INSIDE EDUCATION FOR
PURCHASING MGR., BUYERS, ETC.

EDUCATE PILOT VENDOR

EDUCATE 20% VENDORS

EDUCATE 80% VENDORS

ORGANIZATION DEFINED

INSIDE EDUCATION
FOR VENDOR SCHEDULERS

CUTOVER 20% VENDORS

PHASE 1 — PRODUCTION ITEMS ONLY

Figure 6-2

very high that a company implementing vendor scheduling will have to design and program its vendor schedule and possibly other reports.

That's the bad news. The good news is that many MRP II software packages do contain the ability to maintain purchasing and vendor-related data. The programming task, therefore, becomes one of primarily "retrieval and display" programming, typically less difficult than starting from scratch.

The first tool to address is the vendor schedule itself. Purchasing will have to answer questions such as: What will the format look like? How many weeks are going to be displayed to the vendors? Will capacity units of measure for vendors be included? Will the report display the information horizontally (from the left side to the right side of the vendor schedule), or vertically (top to bottom)? Chapter 2 showed a horizontal format for a vendor schedule. Similar information, but in a vertical format, is shown in Figure 6-3.

The advantage of the vertical format is that it can display an unlimited number of weeks into the future, whereas a horizontal format is somewhat more limited in the number of weeks shown. A potential disadvantage of the vertical format is that it may reduce one's ability to quickly see all the items due from a vendor in a given week. Purchasing must make these decisions early enough to allow the systems and data processing

JONES COMPANY VENDOR SCHEDULE FOR:
SMITH, INC. WEEK OF 02/01/84

VENDOR SCHEDULER: AB   BUYER: CD

	ORDER STATUS	DATE DUE	QUANTITY
PART NUMBER 13579 PLATE	Scheduled	02/01/84	100
LEAD TIME 4 WEEKS	Scheduled	02/22/84	100
	Planned	03/08/84	100
	Planned	05/10/84	100
	Planned	07/12/84	100
PART NUMBER 24680 PANEL	Scheduled	03/01/84	50
LEAD TIME 6 WEEKS	Planned	04/19/84	50
	Planned	06/28/84	50

Figure 6-3

people time to program, test, and debug the vendor schedule.

The second tool needed covers the vendor measurement reports (discussed in detail in Chapter 7). Questions to be answered include: How is the company going to measure delivery, quality, and price? How often does purchasing want the measurement reports and what should they look like? Are both vendors and buyers going to be measured? How about the vendor schedulers? How long should data be kept? Which of this information should be accessible by CRT?

Finally, purchasing needs management tools for use once MRP II and vendor scheduling are "up and running." These can include negotiation reports, purchase commitment reports, and perhaps other supporting information to allow purchasing people to be effective negotiators and buyers. Several examples follow.

On the sample negotiation report, shown in Figure 6-4, all the items in the commodity group are displayed in a descending dollar sequence. It shows the annual usage in dollars, the average weekly usage, the safety stock and lot size information, the current on-hand inventory, and the total dollars used annually in that commodity. This gives the buyer good information to allow him to negotiate annual contracts and manage that commodity effectively. This negotiation information could also be shown by vendor, by plant, etc.

Figure 6-5 shows a typical purchasing commitment report. This report takes the scheduled receipts (shown as an *) and the planned orders (shown as a P) and dollarizes those orders in the week they are due from the vendor. The right-hand column indicates to the buyer the total dollars committed to each vendor over the next 13 weeks. The bottom total indicates the total dollars committed to all vendors in a given week. This aids the buyer in managing his vendor commitments, his future inventory dollars, and the company's requirement for cash flow weekly to support his purchases.

The preceding two examples are just that. Many other kinds of information are available, and the implementation challenge here is to define specifically what's needed and with what frequency.

Negotiation report by commodity code
commodity code 01 and buyer code 80

Part	Description	Safety Stock Wks.	Safety Stock Qty.	Lot Size Wks.	Lot Size Qty.	On-Hand Invent. Wks.	On-Hand Invent. Amt.	Unit Cost	Annual Usage	Avg. Wkly. Usage
896890009	FIBERGLAS	1	75	1	75	1	$767	$ 7.67	$32,704	82
896890008	FIBERGLAS		5		15		$ 0	$13.50	$16,848	24
896890006	FIBERGLAS	5	25	5	25	7	$135	$ 3.87	$ 1,006	5

TOTAL ———— $902 ———— $50,558

Figure 6-4

Defining the Organization

A clear definition of the vendor scheduling organization is also necessary. Following the selection of the vendor scheduling supervisor, it's necessary to establish the reporting structure of the vendor scheduling group. As we stated in Chapter 3, we feel it's preferable to have this group report to purchasing, all things being equal. However, all things are not always equal. Existing organizational structures, geography, the personalities and preferences of people, and other factors may play a part in this decision.

Following this decision, job descriptions for both the buyers and vendor schedulers should be developed. The responsibilities of both the vendor scheduler and buyer, as discussed in the earlier chapters, should be clearly defined in the individual job descriptions. Finally, the vendor schedulers should be selected by month 8 so their purchasing education and training can start the following month.

Vendor Education

MRP II education can't be limited only to the people employed by the company. Vendors are key to the success of any vendor scheduling system, and therefore they need to understand MRP II. Education and training is vital for them.

We recommend bringing vendors into the plant for a one-day vendor education program whenever practical.[2] It's important to have several people present from a given vendor. We recommend that vendor attendees include their customer service/order entry manager, the manager of their scheduling group, and perhaps the

[2] In some cases, due perhaps to geography or other factors, it may be necessary to "take the show on the road"—that is, to conduct the education day at the vendor's plant. This approach can work well, although bringing the vendors into one's own plant seems to have more overall impact and generate better results.

PURCHASING COMMITMENT
BY VENDOR
FOR WEEK ENDING 01/21/XX

DATE 01/19/XX

(*) SCHEDULED RECEIPTS
(P) PLANNED ORDERS

VENDOR		CURRENT & PAST DUE	1/28	2/04	2/11	2/18	2/25	NEXT 4 WEEKS	FOLLOWING 4 WEEKS	VENDOR TOTAL
SMITH COIL	*	2,975.50	743.00	100.50	1,772.50	525.00				6,116.50
EZ	P						575.00	6,683.00	3,199.75	10,457.75
WILSON PLASTICS	*	388.36	1,431.10							1,819.46
FA	P			907.10	908.10	1,254.27	461.21	4,655.20	3,787.37	11,973.25
P B PECK	*	4,880.28	6,002.00	11,851.60	10,087.80	5,281.55				38,103.23
FB	P			1,467.30	1,164.68	1,849.74	8,052.28	44,064.24	40,538.33	97,136.57
HARTMAN	*	2,193.01								2,193.01
FD	P							1,737.60	1,685.60	3,423.20
TODSON	*	5,442.90	6,550.00	4,987.50	135.05	430.00				17,545.45
FE	P				5,435.95	4,988.35	5,675.40	29,272.01	36,917.51	82,289.22
JAMES	*	3,838.85	4,215.20	1,951.00	2,731.00	1,988.40				14,724.45
FF	P						925.00	5,687.00	8,172.74	14,784.74
TOTAL ALL VENDORS		19,718.90	18,941.30	21,265.00	22,235.08	16,317.31	15,688.89	92,099.05	94,301.30	300,566.83

Figure 6-5

plant manager in addition to the local salesman. Even with this, it's a very practical matter to educate a number of vendors in one day.

The vendor education program should consist of basic education on the principles of MRP II, plus more specific training on the vendor scheduling process itself. The agenda for the vendor education day should be developed by around month 10.

Also during that period, it's necessary to develop a vendor education manual. This is a document created especially for the vendors to take back to their companies for use in educating their own employees. It should cover the fundamentals of MRP II, how the vendor schedule works, what's required of the vendor (on-time delivery, quality, for example), the principle of "silence is approval," etc.

Here's an example of how an effective vendor education day might be structured. The first several hours of the morning are devoted to general MRP II education, using some of the same material (videotape plus training aids) used to educate the buyers and vendor schedulers. This session should cover the following topics: fundamentals and applications of MRP II, the mechanics of executing the purchasing plan, and how to operate MRP II in purchasing.

For the balance of the morning, the emphasis would shift to the vendor schedule. The discussion should cover what the vendor schedule looks like, what vendors are authorized to produce (scheduled receipts), how they can plan raw material and capacity, capacity units of measure, and so on. This would also be a good time to verify lead times, lot sizes, minimum order quantities, order quantity multiples above the minimum order quantity, and maximum weekly vendor capacities on each item number, vendor plans for vacation shutdowns, etc.

The agenda for the morning session should also allow time to discuss what day of the week the vendor schedule would be sent to the vendor, cutoff dates for the previous week's receipts, and the need for feedback on past-due orders. The principle of "silence is approval" should also be stressed during this time. Vendors must understand they will be held accountable for delivery on the dates shown on the vendor schedule and that it's *imperative* they communicate in advance that they will miss a delivery date.

After lunch, the first couple of hours in the afternoon should be used to review the vendor manual. Since this is the document the vendors will use to educate their people back home, they must thoroughly understand what's in the vendor manual. As mentioned earlier, this manual should cover MRP, how the vendor schedule works, and what's required of vendors.

The vendor education day should be completed with a commitment from the vendor to work to the vendor schedule, and the development of an action plan to bring performance on delivery and quality up to acceptable levels. Vendors must realize they will now be receiving valid need dates, and therefore that they must ship high-quality parts on time consistently. The action plan would spell out the vendor's current performance levels on delivery and quality. A timetable should be developed showing when the vendor would be at acceptable levels of performance in the areas of delivery and quality to support the vendor scheduling program.

After designing the vendor education program, it's time to do it—to test it with the vendor selected to be the pilot for vendor scheduling (we'll have more to say on this "pilot" approach in the next section). This first "live run" of vendor education should occur by month 11.

Month 12 is spent educating the 20 percent of the vendors who represent 80 percent of the dollars spent on purchased items. Later, beginning in month 14, it's time to educate the remaining 80 percent of the vendors. Once MRP is working on the production items, months 20 through 23 can be devoted to educating the MRO vendors.

By then, all vendors should have been through the initial vendor education day. It's important to schedule follow-up education days with selected vendors who appear not to understand either MRP or the vendor schedule requirements. These follow-up education days would reinforce how the MRP system works and what is required of a vendor receiving the vendor schedule and answer any questions the vendor may have on vendor scheduling.

Pilot and Cutover

At this point, it's time to implement vendor scheduling. In the last chapter, we recommended piloting Master Scheduling and Material Requirements Planning to prove the system is working correctly before cutting over all the items. For the same reasons, we recommended a pilot of vendor scheduling with a selected vendor to be sure it's working correctly before cutting over a large number of vendors.

The best choice for a pilot vendor is a key supplier who is fairly close geographically, well organized, well run, and willing to work with you to develop and perfect your vendor education program and vendor schedule. This key vendor should be selected by month 10 and, as we said earlier, educated in about month 11. This will give purchasing a chance to get feedback on the first vendor education day from the pilot vendor and make changes before educating other vendors.

The actual pilot with the key vendor starts in around month 12 and lasts for three or four weeks—or longer if it's not working properly. (If it's not working, go no further. Stop right there and fix what's wrong.) Based upon the feedback from the pilot vendor, fine tuning of the vendor scheduling system occurs during that period. The measurement reports should also be piloted with the key vendor at the same time.

Here's an important caution: Don't assume vendors will automatically become perfect the minute they start to receive their vendor schedules. It won't happen. Initially, vendors will still have quality and delivery problems. The last thing a company needs when cutting over onto vendor scheduling is to have serious stockouts on purchased items and to shut down production.

It's often a good idea during pilot and cutover to make prudent use of safety stock and/or safety time to protect against vendor problems. Then, as vendor performance improves, these "cushions" can be removed. Remember priority number one when implementing Manufacturing Resource Planning: Run the business.

The 20 percent of the vendors that represent 80 percent of the dollars purchased should be cutover to vendor scheduling beginning in around month 13. During months 13 and 14, you should be able to begin seeing the improved results of having the pilot vendor and the larger vendors on the system. By this time, better on-time delivery, lower inventory, reduced lead times, etc. should start to appear. If these results aren't occurring, something is wrong, either with the vendor schedule itself or the education program. Again, should this happen, go no further. Fix what's wrong before proceeding.

When you begin to see some results, you can begin to cut over the 80 percent of the vendors who represent the last 20 percent of the dollars purchased on production items. This cutover would occur beginning in around month 15, with all production items on vendor scheduling ideally by month 18.

During months 16 through 18, companies should be measuring results with all vendors. They should determine which vendors are not improving their performance on delivery and quality during the first three months. These vendors need follow-up education. Goals for all of these vendors should be established on delivery and quality and action plans established to get them up to acceptable levels of performance in the areas of delivery and quality. The vendor should be in agreement with these goals and action plans and commit to them in writing.

MRO Items

With all the production items on vendor scheduling by around month 18, MRO items can be cut over during months 19 through 24. (See Figure 6-6.)

The detailed plans to add MRO items to the vendor scheduling system should be established by month 19. Operating supplies can be added to the bills of material by month 20, with vendor scheduling of these supplies starting in month 21. Bills of material for preventive maintenance items could be developed during month 22, and the preventive maintenance schedule structured in such a way that it becomes in effect "the master production schedule"

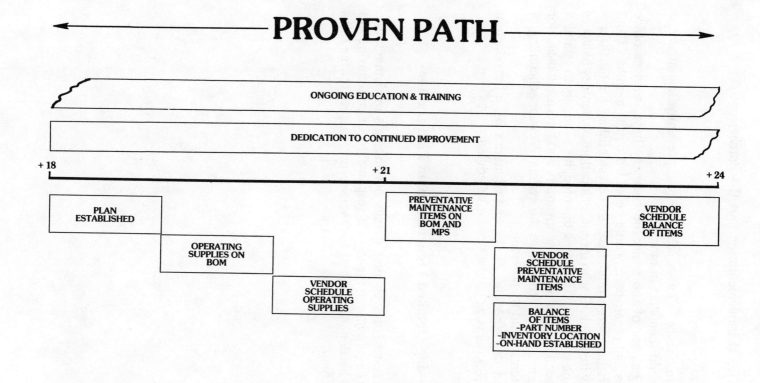

PROVEN PATH

ONGOING EDUCATION & TRAINING

DEDICATION TO CONTINUED IMPROVEMENT

+ 18   + 21   + 24

PLAN ESTABLISHED

OPERATING SUPPLIES ON BOM

VENDOR SCHEDULE OPERATING SUPPLIES

PREVENTATIVE MAINTENANCE ITEMS ON BOM AND MPS

VENDOR SCHEDULE PREVENTATIVE MAINTENANCE ITEMS

BALANCE OF ITEMS
–PART NUMBER
–INVENTORY LOCATION
–ON-HAND ESTABLISHED

VENDOR SCHEDULE BALANCE OF ITEMS

PHASE II — MRO ITEMS

Figure 6-6

for maintenance. Vendor scheduling of preventive maintenance parts could then start in month 23.

The balance of the items the company buys, such as office supplies and repair parts, could be added during months 23 and 24. Part numbers would have to be established for all the remaining items, along with inventory locations. Inventory balances should be verified. Also during this time, it's necessary to establish the desired minimum on-hand inventory and forecasted usage for each item and load them into the system. Vendor scheduling of those items could then begin.

Given this schedule, by the end of month 24, all production and MRO items would be vendor scheduled.

Purchasing Detailed Implementation Plan Outline

The rest of this chapter details purchasing's implementation plan. The purchasing manager is responsible for customizing this plan to his department and assigning responsibilities for the tasks in that plan.

PURCHASING DETAILED IMPLEMENTATION PLAN

TASK	DATE

1. Outside Education

A. Purchasing manager—MRP II class as a part of first-cut education — 1

B. Other key purchasing people—MRP II class — 3

C. Purchasing manager, other key people to class on MRP in purchasing — 3

D. Supervisor of vendor scheduling—MRP II class — 4

E. Supervisor of vendor scheduling—MRP in purchasing class — 5

2. Inside Education

A. Purchasing manager—8-week internal video-based education, the series of business meetings, along with all other department managers — 3–4

B. All purchasing staff, buyers, and vendor scheduling supervisor—internal education, the series of business meetings, with purchasing manager as discussion leader — 5–8

C. Vendor schedulers—internal education, the series of business meetings, with vendor scheduling supervisor as discussion leader — 9–12

3. Specify the Tools

A. 1. Design the vendor schedule — 9

   2. Vendor schedule due from systems group — 10

B. 1. Design measurement reports—delivery, quality, price — 9

   2. Reports due from systems group — 12

C. 1. Design management reports—negotiation report, purchase commitment report, other supporting reports — 9

   2. Reports due from systems group — 14

PURCHASING DETAILED IMPLEMENTATION PLAN

TASK	DATE
4. Organization Defined	
A. Supervisor of vendor scheduling selected	4
B. Reporting structure defined—department to which vendor scheduling group reports established	5
C. Job descriptions developed for buyers and vendor schedulers	6
D. Vendor schedulers selected	8
5. Vendor Education	
A. Agenda for vendor education	10
1. Teaching materials selected	
2. Vendor education manual developed	
3. Vendor commitment and action plan developed	
B. Pilot vendor selected	10
C. Pilot vendor education with key vendor	11
D. Education of the 20 percent of the vendors that represent 80 percent of the dollars	12
E. Educate balance of production item vendors	13–14
F. Educate MRO vendors	20–23
6. Pilot and Cutover	
A. Pilot with key vendor and fine tune the system	12
B. Cut over 20 percent of the vendors that represent 80 percent of the volume (provided pilot is satisfactory)	13
C. Measure results	
1. Pilot measurement reports	12–13
2. Measure results—pilot and 20 percent of the vendors	13–14
D. Cut over remaining vendors—production items only	15–18
E. Measure results for all vendors	16–18
1. Follow-up education—specific vendors	18
2. Goals and action plans for all vendors established and signed off by vendors	18

PURCHASING DETAILED IMPLEMENTATION PLAN

TASK	DATE

7. MRO Items Added to MRP II

   A. Plan established — 19
      1. Operating supplies
      2. Preventive maintenance items
      3. Balance of the items

   B. Operating supplies added to bill of material — 20
   C. Vendor scheduling of operating supplies — 21
   D. Preventive maintenance bill of materials developed and master production schedule established — 22
   E. Vendor scheduling of preventive maintenance parts — 23
   F. Balance of items—office supplies, repair parts, etc. — 23–24
      1. Establish item numbers — 23
      2. Establish inventory location and on-hand balances — 23
      3. Establish desired on-hand inventory and forecasted usage for each item and load to MRP — 23
      4. Vendor schedule balance of items — 24

Chapter 7

Management Information and Measurements

There are three keys to success for MRP II in purchasing. The first is the vendor schedule, which displays the purchased requirements to the vendor. The second is the vendor scheduler, who does the actual Material Requirements Planning and handles routine communications with the vendor, thereby freeing up the buyer's time so he can spend money well. The third key is the set of measurement reports that monitor performance to the plan and provide future visibility.

If MRP II is working correctly, need dates are being displayed to the vendor by means of the vendor schedule. If education has been done properly, users should start noticing a marked improvement in vendor performance. The only way to be absolutely certain of real progress, however, is to measure that performance.

The first step is to establish objective measurements. The buyer should sit down with the vendor, set realistic goals, and develop a timetable for reaching them. It's also important to develop a buyer performance measurement system that, for buyers, highlights differences in performance quickly.

Companies often need to make some basic changes in the way they reward performance. For example, if two buyers receive the same percentage pay raise at year's end, when one had vendors 70 percent on time and the other 98 percent on time, the incentive to perform well is diminished. Compensation systems, therefore, should reward people for good performance. This same principle is equally applicable to vendors. If the 70 percent on-time vendor gets the same percentage of the business as the 98 percent on-time vendor, there is little motivation to work harder. Both buyers and vendors must realize they are expected to meet certain standards. They should be made aware of the unpleasant consequences of poor performance.

Goals should reflect current realities. If a company has just begun measurement reporting, and finds a particular vendor's on-time delivery performance is 70 percent, it's neither fair nor realistic to expect him to achieve 95 percent by the next month. Measurements are a starting point—they help people learn *how* to improve performance by establishing achievable timetables to reach the goal. Then progress toward it should be monitored. Measurement reporting represents an opportunity to develop a better understanding between the vendor and the customer of each other's needs. In this way, they can be used as a basis for improved performance. If measurements are viewed simply as a punishment/reward tool in vendor relationships, the results may be just the opposite of those desired.

How Results Are Measured

A comprehensive performance measurement system covers seven different areas. They are:

- Delivery
- Quality
- Price
- Lead times
- Inventory investment
- Schedule completions in the plant
- Cost reduction/value analysis

Some companies may already be measuring other areas as well. If so, fine. They should be combined with the seven discussed here to provide overall pictures of vendor, buyer, and vendor scheduler performance.

Delivery

Because the company is displaying need dates rather than due dates on its schedule, the vendor *must* deliver on time or a shortage will probably result. The vendor, the buyer, and the vendor scheduler must all realize that the dates on the vendor schedule are "drop dead" dates. Some companies tell their vendors a shipment will be considered "on time" if it arrives anytime from seven days before the due date to seven days after it. That tells the vendor the need dates are *at least* seven days later than the due dates. Performance can't be measured honestly when an order shipped five days late is considered on time. In this situation, it's preferable to allow vendors to ship up to two weeks early. This still provides the same two-week delivery window as the "seven days early or seven days late" policy but without violating the validity of the need date.

If the trucking time for shipping a product varies between three days and ten days, purchasing can instruct the vendor to ship it ten days before the need date. Then it will always arrive on time (before the need date). The buyer should also define the past due cutoff date. If the order is due on Wednesday afternoon, the vendor must realize a Thursday morning delivery will be considered past due. If the order is for 5,000 and the vendor ships only 2,000, the remainder of the order is also considered past due on Thursday morning. Vendors must realize companies are serious when they say an order must arrive on time. Once the ground rules for on-time delivery have been established, performance can be measured more objectively.

It may also be necessary to change the way on-time performance is calculated. Typically, in companies without vendor scheduling, on-time delivery performance is measured by adding up all past due purchase orders and dividing that number by the total number of open purchase orders.

Unfortunately, this measurement technique has some major flaws: It's far too general and doesn't reflect how well a specific buyer did in a particular week or month. Consider this example: If 100 of 1,000 orders are past due, performance would be

90 percent on time. If the vendor's lead times were to increase, the buyer would need to release more orders further in the future. Using this example, there may now be 1,200 open orders. At the same time, the on-time measurement would increase to 92 percent (100 divided by 1,200). Is that because the vendor and the buyer are performing better? Of course not. Obviously, this technique does not provide a true measure of performance.

Here's another example: A buyer has five open orders, each for 20 pieces, with a vendor (Figure 7-1). One of those orders is past due, so the vendor is 80 percent on time.

Current Date 7/1

Due Date	6/25	7/5	7/15	7/25	8/5
Quantity	20	20	20	20	20

Figure 7-1

On July 10, the vendor ships the 20 pieces due on June 25 (Figure 7-2). However, the July 5 shipment is now past due and another order, due August 15, is added. The vendor is again 80 percent on time, because one is late out of five that are due.

Current Date 7/10

Due Date	7/5	7/15	7/25	8/5	8/15
Quantity	20	20	20	20	20

Figure 7-2

On July 20, the vendor ships the 20 pieces due on July 5 (Figure 7-3). The order due July 15 goes past due and another order due on August 25 is added. Looking at the open order report of July 20, the vendor is once again 80 percent on time.

Current Date 7/20

Due Date	7/15	7/25	8/5	8/15	8/25
Quantity	20	20	20	20	20

Figure 7-3

The problem with this is clear: The vendor has shipped every single order late and, in fact, is 0 percent on time in terms of delivery. A delivery measurement system must measure *true* on-time performance. The system should track the receipt date against the due date on the vendor schedule and give the buyer and vendor an objective score on performance against the schedule for that week or month.

Figure 7-4 shows an example of a format for such a measurement report. The buyer and the vendor would go over the report each month. Orders considered past due would be displayed below the totals column for the vendor's review. The principle of "silence is approval" applies. Unless the vendor disagrees with the monthly performance percentage, he is held accountable for it. Since each item is tied to a buyer, a vendor scheduler, and one or more vendors, a similar measurement report could be generated for each of these people.

Reliable delivery is critical to MRP II. Since the vendor schedule is based on need dates, the goal should be a minimum of 95 percent on-time delivery. Now that vendors are receiving the information they need to plan capacity and raw materials via the vendor schedule, they can reasonably be expected to meet the dates. Those starting out at 70 percent on time should set intermediate goals of 80 percent, then 90 percent, and then 95 percent. But, *don't stop there*. Ninety-five percent should be considered as the *minimum acceptable level of performance*. Why not 98 percent or 99 percent? Why not 100 percent?

The delivery measurement report will give purchasing the in-

ABC Supply Company
Month of July

Scheduled Receipts Due	125	
Scheduled Receipts Past Due	1	
On-Time Performance	99.2%	
Order Past Due	200 Part #147	Due 7/15, received 7/22

Figure 7-4

formation needed to identify the problem vendors or items. When those problems are resolved, performance can be expected to improve. The challenge then is to make continuing improvement a way of life. The challenge is to get better and better. Some companies today are achieving nearly 100 percent delivery performance from their vendors. They didn't get there overnight; it's taken lots of hard work on the part of many people. But it's certainly worth it.

The survey in Appendix B indicates that Class A/B MRP II companies using vendor scheduling averaged 97 percent on-time vendor delivery performance. The average company took six months from start of vendor scheduling to accomplish 97 percent on-time delivery performance.

Quality

Out-of-specification parts can represent just as many headaches as parts that arrive late. Again, because vendor scheduling deals with need dates, the items must be of acceptable quality when they arrive at the receiving dock. Companies need to work with their vendors to help them adopt quality control procedures that will assure quality items every time. Obviously their vendors need to have the necessary tools, test equipment, and fixtures to make a quality item. Well-defined specifications on every item and a written agreement to those specifications from the vendor are necessary. But, even having done all that, the company will still need to be assured of incoming purchased part quality.

One way to gain this assurance is via source inspection: to have all vendors certified on quality and doing a complete job of inspecting their output. However, until a company has achieved this status with all of its vendors, it will need formal and objective measurements of the quality level of purchased items coming in the door, as follows.

When a shipment is received, quality control should pull and inspect a sample of that shipment. Based on this inspection, a lot will either be accepted or rejected. The quality measurement would include a record of the number of defective parts and the

**ABC Company
Month of July**

	Samples Pulled	Defective	%	Reason
Part #127	100	3	97	Grease
Part #213	150	3	98	Rust
Part #543	50	3	94	Color
Monthly Total	300	9	97%	

Figure 7-5

type of defect. For example, suppose an inspector pulls 100 samples from an incoming shipment of 1,000 parts and three are found to be defective for various reasons. In this case, the shipment is 97 percent in specification. Every shipment that arrives on the receiving dock would be inspected in this way. The results are recorded against the particular vendor that produced the shipment and summarized weekly or monthly (see Figure 7-5).

In this way, companies can identify the parts or vendors that are consistently a problem. Then they have the option either to improve the performance of the current vendors or find alternative ones. The goal is to have a minimum of 98 percent of all items within specification so the plant can adhere to their schedules consistently.

One last point: Rejected shipments should not count as on-time shipments. A rejected lot means the vendor gets a bad grade not only on quality but also on delivery (unless the lot can be reworked prior to the scheduled date).

Price

Few companies measure price performance for each vendor and buyer to find out who is doing a good job of controlling costs and who isn't. While many buyers can boast of their cost reduction programs, few can talk about the total impact of all price increases and decreases on the bottom line of the profit and loss statement.

Is pricing, delivery, or quality a company's most important measurement of performance? For many companies, delivery and quality are probably more critical than price. It's far better to purchase in uneconomical quantities and keep the shop running than to get a "real buy" and shut the line down waiting for delivery. But price is still an important factor if a company is to remain competitive, so it's vital to measure performance in all three areas.

Many companies measure price against a standard cost. In these cases, the price measurement is actually more of a reflection of how well the standard was established than of how wisely the buyers are using the company's financial resources. Suppose that, on January 1, a vendor's price is $1. Purchasing estimates an 8 percent inflation factor, so the estimated cost at the end of the year would be $1.08. If the standard cost was calculated as the average cost for the year, purchasing would place the standard cost at $1.04. However, if purchasing guessed wrong and the inflation factor was really 10 percent, the buyer's price performance would likely show an unfavorable variance of 2 percent at the end of the year. The buyer has little or no control over this factor.

We feel it's preferable to measure actual performance rather than against a standard cost. It's much fairer to the buyers to measure them in a way that takes into account all the price increases and decreases and gives a weighted price index of performance. That price index, calculated for each item, is shown in Figure 7-6.

Each item would be calculated the same way and the total summed by buyer or by vendor (Figure 7-7). Using this technique, purchasing has an objective measure of price performance for each buyer and vendor. Now it's possible to determine that Ven-

Price at end of year	$1.06
Price at start of year	1.00
Difference	.06
Annual Usage	10,000
Annual Price Impact	+ $600.00

Figure 7-6

Part #	Price EOY	Price SOY	Difference	Annual Quantity	Annual $	Price Impact
137	1.06	1.00	.06	10,000	$10,000	+$600
243	.47	.45	.02	100,000	45,000	+2000
549	.03	.03	—	10,000	300	—
637	.63	.67	.04	6,000	4,020	−240
					$59,320	+$2360
					Price Index	104

Figure 7-7

dor A (80 percent on time, 80 percent within specification, and 112 percent on the price index) is not as good as Vendor B (who is 98 percent on time, 97 percent within specification, and 103 percent on the price index). The same principle is equally applicable to buyers.

Lead Times

As we discussed earlier, vendor scheduling allows companies to reduce their lead times significantly. Basically, vendor scheduling represents a change from "paper" lead times to true manufacturing lead times. As the vendor learns to use the information available to him in the vendor schedule to do a better job of planning raw materials and capacity, he will feel more comfortable working to manufacturing lead times. Purchasing should measure lead times regularly to see how well their vendors understand the system. If the desired results aren't being achieved, more education may be necessary for the vendor or buyer involved.

Purchasing can measure two areas regarding lead times. First, of all the items purchased, how many have shorter lead times than before MRP II implementation? Once vendor scheduling is working, this answer should approach 100 percent. The second measurement would be the percentage of reduction in lead times. This would vary from company to company, depending upon the commodities purchased, but the result should be fairly substantial in most companies.

In Appendix B, several examples of lead time reductions are cited. All those companies surveyed reported substantial lead time reductions.

Inventory Investment/Inventory Turnover

Since purchasing is able to bring in the items to true *need* dates, rather than to invalid due dates, substantial inventory reductions are possible. The Class A/B users of MRP II surveyed reported they typically saw a 25 percent reduction in purchased part inventory levels—in the face of substantial inflation and, in many of the companies, high growth.

Schedule Completions in the Plant

One key test of the success of any MRP II implementation is customer service: the number of orders being shipped complete and on time. That number should be measured weekly to ensure all departments are executing the schedule correctly. The plant is a "customer" of purchasing, so measuring purchasing's performance amounts to measuring the "customer service" which purchasing is providing to the plant. Similarly the sales department is the "customer" of the plant, and the plant should be measured accordingly; its "customer service" measure is performance to the master production schedule.

Some of the best Class A MRP II companies publish weekly their scheduled completions by product line. If a date is missed, it's recorded, as is the reason for the delay. This leads to identifying the root cause of the problem and solving it. Things that get measured get better. Do it right the first time.

Cost Reduction/Value Analysis

Purchasing should establish cost reduction/value analysis goals for each buyer and measure him against those goals. MRP II helps the buyer in this area by identifying the items with the biggest annual savings potential. Purchasing can extract the annual usage of each item from the MRP II system and dollarize it. Then, by printing the list of all the buyer's items in descending dollar order, the buyer can concentrate his effort on those items with the greatest potential payback. Purchasing should measure the dollars saved against the goals set and routinely publish the results.

Intangible Results

Many intangible benefits can be derived from MRP II in purchasing. First, there is improved credibility. When the vendor scheduler tells the vendor he needs an item on a certain date, the vendor believes it because he understands the MRP II system. When purchasing tells the plant an item will arrive at 8:00 A.M. on Wednesday, they believe it, and on Tuesday night, they set up the equipment to run it.

There's also the improvement in quality of life. Purchasing has valid data to work with and knows what is expected. Buyers have retired the old "fire truck" and are out in front, managing their commodities. The vendors are communicating to the company in advance of a problem so there's time to work out alternative solutions. Everyone is part of the same team and recognized for his contributions.

Third, the purchasing department becomes more motivated and professional. With time to perform the really important parts of their jobs, buyers are more valuable to the company. They save the company money because they are negotiating contracts and tracking costs, instead of putting out fires. Using the future visibility provided by MRP II, the buyer can make better decisions and take actions that will have very positive long-term effects.

Chapter 8

Just-in-Time in Purchasing

There's been a great deal written and discussed recently regarding Just-in-Time. And that's good news, because Just-in-Time represents an excellent set of tools.

The bad news is that much of what's been said has generated confusion rather than clarity, questions rather than understanding, apprehension rather than enthusiasm. Consequently, many purchasing people have become reluctant to investigate the potential of Just-in-Time for their operations, and that's too bad.

Just-in-Time, when done properly, can generate enormous benefits in purchasing, in the plant, and in other parts of the company. But just like any other tool (MRP II's a good example), it can be misapplied, misdirected, or used in a half-baked manner. And then the expected results just won't be there.

Consider an individual named Bill (or Margaret or Harry), the purchasing manager in a manufacturing company operating in 'order launch and expedite mode.'' His daily work life is replete with the kinds of problems we pointed out back in Chapter 1: convoluted communications, conflicts with production and inventory control over price versus quantity, mountains of paperwork, ludicrously long lead times, not enough hours in the day to do his job because of the expediting monkey on his back.

One fine day Bill gets a phone call from his boss's boss, the general manager. He's calling from the Orient, and he's very enthused. He says, ''Bill, I'm on a fact-finding tour of Japan. What these people are doing is super! Have Just-in-Time implemented with all your vendors by the time I get back.''

At that point, Bill may be going under for the third time. Bill, in fact, may be the purchasing manager who first uttered the phrase, ''We don't do Just-in-Time in our purchasing department.

We do 'just-in-case.' We buy some of everything and pray we don't run out."

Just-in-Time is:

• not a quick fix. It takes time and hard work to create the environment to make Just-in-Time succeed.

• not Kanban. Kanban (defined in Appendix G, Glossary) is a technique to schedule certain activities in a Just-in-Time environment. There's a great deal more to Just-in-Time than Kanban.

• not something to push off on vendors and ignore internally. Just-in-Time needs to work in the *inside* factory, as well as the ones outside.

• not culturally and/or geographically dependent. Just-in-Time is being operated very successfully in North America and Europe by non-Orientals, many of whom have never been west of Hawaii or east of the Iron Curtain.

• not primarily an inventory reduction program. As with MRP II, lower inventories are one result of Just-in-Time but are not the primary objective.

• not a "computerless" system. Except for extremely small companies, we're not aware of anyone doing a good job of Just-in-Time without substantial computer support.

What is it, then, this thing called Just-in-Time? Here's a workable definition, perhaps not as comprehensive as some would like, but more than adequate for our purposes:

Just-in-Time is an approach to achieving excellence in a manufacturing company based on the continuing elimination of waste and consistent improvement in productivity. Waste is defined as those things which do not add value to the product.

Yes indeed . . . the continuing elimination of waste and ongoing improvement in productivity.

In one sense, Just-in-Time is a methodology for solving problems:

- As Just-in-Time takes hold, the inventories start to drop.
- As inventories drop, the problems become more visible. (It's a bit like draining the swamp, thereby making more visible the rocks and stumps and possibly the alligators.)
- Once problems are identified, they can be solved.
- As problems are solved, the inventories can be lowered even further, thereby uncovering more problems and exposing them to solutions.

Just-in-Time, buying and making only what one needs just when one needs it, implies very small order quantities. Only one or three or five of a given item may be needed. However, that item traditionally may have a fixed order quantity, a vendor minimum, or perhaps a price break at 10 or 30 or perhaps 300 units.

The reason for the larger order quantity? As we said earlier, it's generally there to amortize the setup costs over a larger number of items. The Just-in-Time approach challenges the setup time (hence costs) and rightly so. It recognizes an important factor, which we'll call axiom #1:

As set-up costs approach zero, order quantity can approach one.

However, there's a bit more to it than setups. It's possible to drive setup times to near zero, but still not be able to run efficiently with one-for-one order quantities. The potential culprit: inspection costs, caused, of course, by having to inspect many more orders, albeit smaller ones. Hence axiom #2:

As inspection costs approach zero, order quantity can approach one.

But there's more. One could have short setups and low inspection costs and still have a problem with transportation. Too many LTL (less-than-truckload) shipments means too high a freight bill, which is exactly opposite of the objective. Hence axiom #3:

As incremental transportation costs approach zero, order quantity can approach one.

Please note the word "incremental." Obviously, transportation costs will never get close to zero. What we're talking about here is the avoidance of *additional* freight costs resulting from smaller and more frequent shipments.

There are, to be sure, many other factors which bear on the totality of Just-in-Time, such as preventive maintenance, worker involvement, good housekeeping, standardized containers, and on and on. However, for the purposes of our discussion here, we'd like to concentrate on four key elements: scheduling (including the setup issue), quality, transportation, and leadership by example.

Scheduling

Just-in-Time, as we said earlier, means buying and producing only *what one needs* just *when one needs it.* To do this, obviously, requires knowing *what's needed* and *when*—accurately, consistently, routinely—and this means valid schedules. If a company can't schedule well, it can't do Just-in-Time effectively. It may get some benefits from a Just-in-Time program, but not nearly what it could. Therefore, at the risk of stating the obvious, we point out that *Just-in-Time requires valid schedules of what's needed and when.*

In virtually all manufacturing companies, the only way to get valid schedules is via MRP/MRP II. There are some companies with an operating environment so simple and so stable that MRP isn't necessary. However, most of the really successful Just-in-Time companies in North America use MRP/MRP II, as do many in Japan.

The basic logic of MRP is the logic of Just-in-Time. MRP with one-for-one lot sizing, short lead times, zero safety stock, and no scrap/shrinkage/yield factors will plan to zero inventory, with replenishment scheduled to be only what's needed just when it's needed. MRP II generates valid plans and schedules, without which Just-in-Time can't really function. Just-in-Time simplifies the environment and executes the schedules very well, which enables MRP II to work even better. From this we can conclude that *MRP II and Just-in-Time are complementary, not contradictory; they work best when they work together.*

In a very real sense, this entire book is about Just-in-Time. Vendor scheduling, as we've seen throughout the book, calls for:

• valid schedules
• long-term relationships with vendors
• open and frequent communications
• a minimum of paperwork.
• etc., etc., etc.

Well, so does Just-in-Time. In effect, Just-in-Time allows a company to build on vendor scheduling, and to go even further and get even better. *Just-in-Time with vendors is a logical and a natural evolution from vendor scheduling.* Note, we didn't say "an easy evolution." It's not. But few truly worthwhile things are easy, and Just-in-Time in purchasing is no exception.

From purely a scheduling standpoint, going to Just-in-Time from vendor scheduling is conceptually not a great leap. In essence, all that might be involved is to express the near-term schedule in time periods smaller than one week, probably in days or fractions of days. See Figure 8-1. The top display, reproduced from Chapter 2, is a traditional type of vendor schedule. The middle part of Figure 8-1 shows the near-term schedule expressed in days, while the lower section displays the schedule in half-day increments.

In the example in Figure 8-1, part #24680 appears to be in constant demand, hence possibly constant production by the vendor. Perhaps Smith Inc., the vendor, has been able to dedicate one or several machines full-time to the production of this item. Hence no ongoing setup costs, which is good news. Hence continuing application of the learning curve. More good news. At this stage the Jones Company might ask itself: "What if we

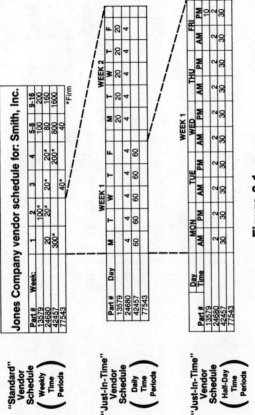

"Standard" Vendor Schedule (Weekly Time Periods)

Jones Company vendor schedule for: Smith, Inc.

Part #	Week: 1	2	3	4	5-8	9-16
13579	20	100*			100	200
24680		20*	20*		80	160
42457	300*			200*	800	1600
77543			40*	200*	40	

*Firm

"Just-In-Time" Vendor Schedule (Daily Time Periods)

Part #	Day	WEEK 1 M	T	W	T	F	WEEK 2 M	T	W	T	F
13579		4	4	4	4	4	20	20	20	20	20
24680		60	60	60	60	60	4	4	4	4	4
42457											
77543											

"Just-In-Time" Vendor Schedule (Half-Day Time Periods)

Part #	Time	MON AM	PM	TUE AM	PM	WED AM	PM	THU AM	PM	FRI AM	PM
13579		2	2	2	2	2	2	2	2	2	10
24680		30	30	30	30	30	30	30	30	30	30
42457											
77543											

Figure 8-1

could modify our master schedule to run continuously the products that use part #13579 and #42457? Then perhaps the folks at Smith Inc. could go into constant production on those." If so, the results could well be less setup, more learning curve, and a better deal for both companies.

This technique, often called "mixed model master scheduling," can yield big benefits. The basic approach is to run some of each product each week, rather than to make long runs of one product, then another, then another.

The objective: to enable the vendors (as well as the internal fabrication centers) to produce in synchronization with the now repetitive master schedule, to achieve the setup and learning curve benefits cited above. A requirement: very low setup and change-over times in the assembly and finishing operations.

Quality

Inspection at the source is a key element of Just-in-Time. One of the reasons for this is to eliminate incoming inspection, thereby driving inspection costs toward zero. For the inside factory, one's own plant, this means things like Statistical Process Control (SPC). This approach monitors the items being produced while they're being produced, adjusting the process when necessary, stopping the process when it can't be kept in control, thereby eliminating separate inspection steps.

For the vendors, SPC may (probably should) be employed in their plants. At a minimum, however, vendors supplying a Just-in-Time company need to inspect their own output and verify its quality so that the company can eliminate the incoming inspection step in its plant and still be *assured* that the quality is there.

Folks, this isn't easy. It doesn't happen overnight. But it is practical and attainable. One large West Coast manufacturer of electronic equipment, as a result of its excellent efforts with MRP II and Just-in-Time, was able to reduce its incoming inspection staff from *one hundred people* down to *one*. That's right, one person. Their position: Separate inspection steps do not add value to the product; hence they qualify as waste; hence they should be eliminated wherever possible.

The quality issue with vendors is one of the tougher nuts to crack in this entire Just-in-Time process. It calls for hard work, massive education of vendors, close working relationships between purchasing and the quality assurance people within the company, vendor certification programs and much more. It also calls for substantial sole sourcing. Most of the successful Just-in-Time companies we know have, as a stated objective, sole-sourcing wherever possible. A major U.S.-based manufacturer of office equipment, also an excellent MRP II/JIT user, was able to reduce its worldwide vendor base from *five thousand* down to *three hundred*. Their main motivation to do this: They felt there was no way that they could work closely enough with five thousand vendors to get the necessary levels of quality. It became a much more practical matter with three hundred.

Sole-sourcing can be controversial and, to some purchasing people, a bit scary. Debates regarding its merits often generate "more heat than light" as the saying goes. At the heart of much of the concern over sole-sourcing is the issue of continuity of supply. What happens, one can ask, if one of our sole-source vendors has a flood, or a fire, or goes on strike?

There's a method which some companies have employed very successfully in this area. Let's take the case of a company buying two parts on a multiple-source basis from three different vendors. The arrangement might look like the one shown in Figure 8-2.

Volume Split

	Volume Split		
	Vendor A	Vendor B	Vendor C
Part #1	60%	30%	10%
Part #2	30%	60%	10%

Figure 8-2

A sole-source arrangement to ensure continuity of supply might be as shown in Figure 8-3.

Volume Split

	Volume Split		
	Vendor A	Vendor B	Vendor C
Part #1	100%	*	0%
Part #2	*	100%	0%

* Qualified as back-up supplier.

Figure 8-3

If Vendor A has a flood, Vendor B pitches in and runs Part #1 until Vendor A can get back up and running. And vice versa with Part #2. Vendor C is dropped from the vendor base, or perhaps becomes the sole source for other parts.

Fewer vendors means a less difficult job for purchasing and quality assurance to get the vendors educated and certified on quality. Fewer vendors means more concentration of volume, which may permit a more constant and repetitive mode of production by the vendors. This, in turn, can enhance the lower setup and learning curve effects mentioned earlier. Fewer vendors also means more opportunities for freight consolidation, and that leads us to the next section.

Transportation

It's possible to do all the good things mentioned above and still come out a loser. The freight bills could be astronomical. Just-in-Time with vendors means many more shipments, and smaller shipments. Transportation, therefore, must be reckoned with.

We've seen essentially three approaches to the transportation issue with Just-in-Time:

1. Relocation of vendor plants.

2. Use of company-owned and -operated vehicles.

3. Freight consolidation.

Frankly we're not very enthusiastic about the first method, relocation of vendor plants. Most companies, even large ones, simply don't have the "clout" to force vendors to build new plants right down the street. Even for those companies that do have that kind of muscle, one can question the economics involved. It may take a very long time for the savings coming solely from proximity to outweigh the costs involved in relocation, hiring, training, start-up, and the amortization of new brick and mortar plus equipment.

The second approach, use of company-owned and -operated vehicles, can be very effective. One company, located in upstate New York, operates what it calls the "bus route." It's actually a company truck, whose driver makes daily pick-ups at vendors within an approximate fifty-mile radius. That's for the vendors nearby. This same company also has a concentration of suppliers in the greater Chicago area, and it operates a "bus route" there also. Each day there's a pick-up at the key Chicago vendors, and less than a day later the parts go right from the truck to the assembly line, which is hundreds of miles from Chicago.

Freight consolidation, the third method, involves the use of public carriers, not only to deliver but to consolidate. The consolidation process involves a variety of vendors delivering their daily output to a central point, typically a carrier's facility. Each day, then, the carrier consolidates these many LTL deliveries into a full truckload and delivers to the customer. Carriers are hungry for this business. Thanks to deregulation, they can now go after it.

A major U.S. computer manufacturer, once again an excellent MRP II/JIT user, has taken this approach with excellent results. In doing so, it has learned to deal with its carriers in a very similar fashion as with its vendors:

- It has fewer carriers. Its carrier base has shrunk dramatically.
- It has recognized the need to educate and train its carriers, as well as its vendors, on Just-in-Time. It conducts vendor education days for the vendors; it also conducts carrier education days for the carriers, to educate and train them on its Just-in-Time approach and related transportation requirements.

Leadership by Example

The moral of this story is "practice what you preach." Don't make the mistake, as some have, of looking upon Just-in-Time as a means of forcing vendors to carry more inventory, incur more setups, do more inspection, and jump through more hoops.

Just-in-Time, when done incorrectly, may actually *increase* waste, inefficiency, and cost, not decrease it. When a company's Just-in-Time program is not much more than a ploy to offload problems and inventories to vendors, it may for a time appear to be working. But, sooner or later, the chickens will come home to roost. The price will be paid, usually in the form of cost increases, lower quality, less responsiveness, and/or vendors declining to renew contracts because they're losing money on the business.

Here are some questions which vendors may ask regarding Just-in-Time:

- How should we go about reducing setups?
- How does one do in-process inspection?
- We're having a problem figuring out how to schedule your volume on a Just-in-Time basis. Can you help us?

- What are Just-in-Time's requirements for preventive maintenance?

- How can we get the level of worker involvement necessary for Just-in-Time?

The purchasing people initiating Just-in-Time with their vendors have, broadly, two ways to respond to these kinds of questions:

We don't know. Figure it out for yourselves. Don't bother us; we're too busy.

or

Come on over to our plant and take a look. We're doing it. We don't have all the answers, but we have some and we're getting a bit smarter every day. We've got some really talented people in production (or manufacturing or engineering or quality or human resources or production control), and they'll be glad to help. If need be, down the road, they can pay a visit to your plant and work directly with more of your people.

It's obvious which is the correct answer. If a company is prepared to lead by example, to do itself what its asking its vendors to do, to help its vendors and to treat them as partners in the Just-in-Time journey, then the results from Just-in-Time will be there. Solid, bottom-line results over and beyond the enormous benefits already generated from MRP II and vendor scheduling.

Chapter 9
The Future

What's next? What's coming down the road? Broadly we see three major trends.

More of the Same Good News

More Manufacturing Resource Planning, more vendor scheduling, more Just-in-Time. These tools, these "philosophies" as they're called by some, are valid, genuine, and here to stay. They'll be implemented by increasing numbers of companies in the future.

Electronic Data Interchange (EDI)

EDI refers to computer-to-computer transmission of vendor schedules. A good example of this happening now is a major automobile company in Japan, not Toyota but a primary competitor. This company, which happens to be a Class A user of MRP II, has a vendor base somewhat geographically dispersed. It maintains that Kanban is too slow for communications because of the distances involved. It communicates its MRP-generated schedules to its vendors electronically, computer-to-computer, in microseconds because Kanban would require a day or more.

It's happening in North America, also. One very large manufacturer of office equipment has over a third of its vendors on EDI and is adding more. This company has valid schedules, thanks to MRP II, and it also has an excellent and very successful Just-in-Time program.

Conceptually, EDI is not a very large leap. MRP generates the schedules, and the vendor scheduler reviews them. At that point, the computer is authorized to transmit the schedule or, alternatively, to make the schedule electronically available for vendor inquiry. This is in lieu of mailing the vendor schedule or sending a Kanban card. It reduces lead time by perhaps an entire day or more; it reduces paperwork; it *reduces waste.*

Closer Relationships Among "Channel Partners"

The total logistics channel, from ultimate raw material to final consumer, typically involves many separate companies: extractors, converters, processors, assemblers, distributors, retailers. These company-to-company interfaces have traditionally been characterized by arms-length and often adversarial relationships, secrecy, price considerations to the exclusion of much else, etc.

This pattern is changing, for the better. The trend is very visible, and it's due, among other things, to MRP II, vendor scheduling, Just-in-Time, and an increased awareness of the need to run manufacturing companies better.

Here's another example, also from the automotive industry, but from the other side of the world—Europe.

Company F manufactures trucks, selling to many different customers in a variety of configurations and optional equipment. One of this company's key vendors is Company C, which produces diesel engines.

Company F does vendor scheduling with Company C. The scheduled receipts and planned orders in Company F's vendor schedule become direct inputs to Company C's master schedule.

Company C also does vendor scheduling with its vendors. It uses its excellent MRP II system to generate schedules for its suppliers in a very similar fashion to its customer, Company F.

Does this work well? Yes, very. Does it work perfectly? No, because not all of Company F's vendors have excellent MRP II systems like Company C. No, because not all of Company C's customers have excellent schedules and do vendor scheduling like Company F. No, because not all of Company C's vendors do vendor scheduling with their suppliers. But, it's working well today and it will continue to work better and better as more and more of these channel partners get with the program.

There are important implications in this for people in purchasing. Purchasing people, and their counterparts in the sales and marketing function, work at the intercompany interfaces. They're the people linkages between channel partners. They spend much of their working time dealing with people from other companies, i.e., their vendors. The need to develop and nurture solid vendor-customer relations is much more obvious today than it was even a few years ago. Therefore, the need for competent, highly professional purchasing people is greater. And, as the importance of intercompany teamwork becomes more and more apparent, the role and stature of purchasing people will be even further enhanced.

Conclusion

One can readily observe:

- More sole-sourcing.
- Shrinking vendor bases.
- Longer-term relationships.
- More communication and sharing of information.
- Distributors doing DRP/vendor scheduling with their suppliers, who are manufacturers and who in turn are doing MRP II/vendor scheduling with their vendors.

All of this is very good news. The friction, the confusion, the safety stock buffers, and the other elements of waste at the intercompany interfaces are beginning to decrease. This trend will continue and will accelerate as channel partners learn to work *as partners*, not adversaries.

As this trend continues to take hold, the entire manufacturing sectors of our economies will operate far more efficiently, far more productively. In North America and elsewhere, we've been reacquiring an appreciation of the critical role of manufacturing and logistics in the overall economy. None too early, but certainly not too late.

Let's get to work. Let's make it happen in purchasing.

Appendix A

The Mechanics of Manufacturing Resource Planning (MRP II)

Section 1
The Closed Loop System

The basic logic of the closed loop MRP II system is extremely simple. It's in every cookbook. The "bill of material" says, "Turkey stuffing takes one egg, seasoning, bread crumbs, etc." The routing says, "Put the egg and the seasoning in a blender." The blender is the work center. The master schedule is Thanksgiving.

But, in manufacturing, there is a lot more volume and a lot more change. There isn't just one product. There are many. The lead times aren't as short as going to the corner store. The work centers are busy rather than waiting for work—because some of them cost a third of a million dollars or more—and it simply is not wise economically to let them sit idle and to have excess capacity. In addition, the sales department will undoubtedly change the date of Thanksgiving several times before it actually arrives! And this isn't through perversity. This is because the customers want and need some things earlier or later.

The volume of activity in manufacturing is monumentally high; something is happening all the time. And change is the norm, not the exception.

But the point is that the *logic* of MRP II is very straightforward indeed. Figure A-1 shows the closed loop system.

The production plan is the *rate* of production for a product family typically expressed in units like, "We want to produce 1,100 Model 30 pumps per week." The production plan is made by taking into account current inventory, deciding whether inventory needs to go up or down during the planning period, projecting the sales forecast, and determining the rate of production required to maintain, raise, or lower the inventory level. For a make-to-order product, as opposed to a make-to-stock product, the "order backlog" rather than the inventory is the starting point for the production plan.

Figure A-2 shows a typical production plan. Figure A-3 shows a business plan which is simply an extension of the production plan into dollars. The complete business plan in a manufacturing company will include research and development and other expenses not directly related to production and purchases. But the core of any business plan in a manufacturing enterprise is the production plan. With MRP II, the production plan and business plan are interdependent and, as the production plan is updated, it is extended into dollars to show it in the common denominator of business—money.

The MRP II system then takes a master schedule ("What are we going to make?"), "explodes" this through the bill of material ("What does it take to make it?"), and compares

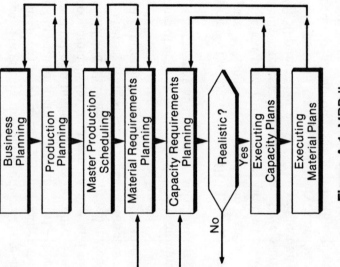

Figure A-1 MRP II

The Mechanics of Closed Loop / 131

this with the inventory on hand and on order ("What do we have?") to determine material requirements ("What do we have to get?").

This fundamental material requirements planning (MRP) logic is shown in Figure A-4. Figure A-5 shows the bill of material. For this example, a small gasoline engine for a moped is the product being manufactured. The bill of material shown in Figure A-5 is what's known as an "indented bill of material." This simply means that the highest level items in the bill of material are shown farthest left. For example, the piston assembly components are "indented" to the right to indicate that they go into that assembly. Therefore, in this example, they are at "level 2."

A bill of material "in reverse" is called a "where-used" list. It would say, for example, that the locating pins go into the crankcase half-left, which goes into the engine.

Month Ending		Sales (thousands)	Production (thousands)	Inventory (thousands)
3/31	Plan			
	Actual			
4/30	Plan	30	35	60
	Actual	25	36	71
6/30	Plan	30	35	65
	Actual			75

Figure A-2 Production Plan

Month Ending		Sales (thousands)	Production (thousands)	Inventory (thousands)
3/31	Plan	3,000	3,500	6,000
	Actual	3,000	3,600	6,500
4/30	Plan	3,000	3,500	7,000
	Actual	2,500	3,600	7,100
5/31	Plan	3,000	3,500	7,000
	Actual	3,800	3,200	6,500
6/30	Plan	3,000	3,500	7,500
	Actual	3,200	3,700	7,000
12/31	Plan	3,000	3,500	10,500
	Actual			

Figure A-3 Business Plan

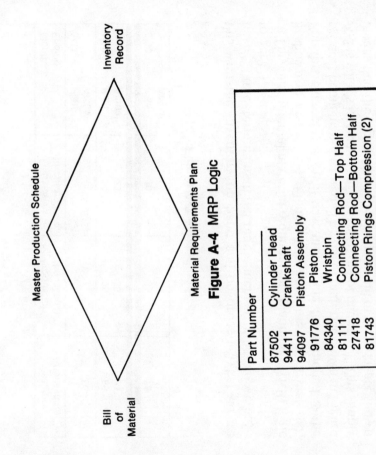

Figure A-4 MRP Logic

Master Production Schedule

Inventory Record

Bill of Material

Material Requirements Plan

Figure A-5 Moped Engine Bill of Material

Part Number	
87502	Cylinder Head
94411	Crankshaft
94097	Piston Assembly
91776	Piston
84340	Wristpin
81111	Connecting Rod—Top Half
27418	Connecting Rod—Bottom Half
81743	Piston Rings Compression (2)
96652	Piston Ring Oil
20418	Bearing Halves (2)
59263	Lock Bolts (2)
43304	Crankcase Half Right
28079	Crankcase Half Left
80021	Locater Pins (2)

Master Production Schedule

Engines

	Week							
	1	2	3	4	5	6	7	8
Master Schedule	80	0	100	0	0	120	0	120
Actual Demand	40	40	30	30	30	40	40	20
Available to Promise	0	0	10	0	0	40	0	100

Figure A-6 Master Production Schedule

Figure A-6 shows a master schedule for engines. In a make-to-stock company, the master schedule would be very similar, but it would take into account the inventory on hand.

Section 2
Material Requirements Planning (MRP)

Figure A-7 shows the material requirements plan for the crankcase half-left and also for the locator pin that goes into the crankcase half-left. The projected gross requirements come from the master schedule plus any service parts requirements. "Scheduled receipts" are the orders that are already in production or out with the vendors. The projected available balance takes the on-hand figure, subtracts requirements from it, and adds scheduled re-

Material Requirements Plan
Crankcase Half — Left

LEAD TIME = 4 WEEKS
ORDER QUANTITY = 200

					Week				
		1	2	3	4	5	6	7	8
Projected Gross Requirements		80	0	100	0	0	120	0	120
Scheduled Receipts				240					
Proj. Avail. Bal.	120	40	40	180	180	180	60	60	120
Planned Order Release					200				-60

Material Requirements Plan
Locater Pin (2 Per)

LEAD TIME = 4 WEEKS
ORDER QUANTITY = 500

					Week				
		1	2	3	4	5	6	7	8
Projected Gross Requirements					400				400*
Scheduled Receipts									
Proj. Avail. Bal.	430	430	430	430	30	30	30	30	-370
Planned Order Release					500				

*Requirements from Another Crankcase

Figure A-7 Material Requirements Plan

ceipts to it. (In Figure A-7, the starting on-hand balance is 120 for the crankcase half-left.) This calculation projects future inventory balances to indicate when material needs to be ordered or rescheduled.

The material on hand and on order subtracted from the gross requirements yields "net requirements" (60 in week 8 for the crankcase half-left in Figure A-8). This is the amount that is actually needed to cover requirements. When the net requirements are converted to lot sizes and backed off over the lead time, they are called "planned order releases."

The "planned order releases" at one level in the product structure—in this case 200 "crankcase half-left"—become the projected gross requirements at the lower level. The 200-unit planned order release in period four for the crankcase half-left becomes a projected gross requirement of 400 locater pins in period four since there are two locater pins per crankcase half-left.

MRP — Rescheduling
Crankcase Half — Left

LEAD TIME = 4 WEEKS
ORDER QUANTITY = 200

	Week							
	1	2	3	4	5	6	7	8
Projected Gross Requirements	80	0	100	0	0	120	0	120
Scheduled Receipts				240				
Proj. Avail. Bal.	120	40	-60	180	180	60	60	-60
Planned Order Release				200				

MRP — Locater Pin (2 Per)

LEAD TIME = 4 WEEKS
ORDER QUANTITY = 500

	Week							
	1	2	3	4	5	6	7	8
Projected Gross Requirements				400				400*
Scheduled Receipts								
Proj. Avail. Bal.	430	430	430	30	30	30	30	-370
Planned Order Release				500				

*Requirements from Another Crankcase

Figure A-8 MRP—Rescheduling

Most MRP systems also include what is called "pegged requirements." This is simply a way to trace where the requirements came from. For example, the pegged requirements for the locater pins would indicate that the 400 in period four came from the crankcase half-left and that the 400 in period eight came from another product. Pegged requirements show the quantity, the time period, and the higher level item where the requirements are coming from.

Figure A-8 shows the same crankcase half as in Figure A-7. Note, however, that now the scheduled receipt is shown in period four. This means that the due date on the shop order or the purchase order is week four. An MRP system would generate a reschedule message for the planner to move the scheduled receipt from week four into week three to cover the requirements in week three.

Note, also, that the fact that the scheduled receipt for the crankcase half needs to be rescheduled does not affect the requirements for locater pins. The locater pins have already been released into production for the crankcase halves that are on order. The "requirements" for locater pins are for planned orders that have *not* been released yet.

The bill of material is the instrument for converting planned order releases at one level into projected gross requirements at a lower level. The bill of material for the crankcase half-left, for example, would show that two locater pins per crankcase half were required.

Section 3
Capacity Planning and Scheduling

Capacity planning for the manufacturing facility follows the same general logic as the material requirements planning shown in Figure A-4. Figure A-9 shows this capacity requirements planning logic. The remaining operations on released shop orders and all of the operations on planned order releases are "exploded" through the routings (like bills of material for operations) and posted against the work centers (like an inventory of capacities). The result is a capacity requirements plan in standard hours by work center showing the number of standard hours required to meet the material requirements plan. This capacity requirements plan shows the capacity that will be required to execute the master schedule, and consequently, the production plan.

It's important to note that everything in an MRP II system is in "lock step." If the capacity to meet the material requirements plan can't be obtained either through a company's own manufacturing facilities, subcontracting, or purchasing material on the outside, obviously the master schedule will have to be changed. But that is the last resort. The objective is to make the master schedule happen.

Operations scheduling involves assigning individual schedule dates to the operations on a shop order using scheduling rules. Scheduling rules would typically be similar to these:

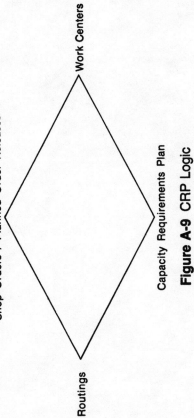

Shop Orders / Planned Order Releases

Routings

Capacity Requirements Plan

Work Centers

Figure A-9 CRP Logic

1. Allow two days for inspection. (This is a matter of judgment.)

2. Round the standard hours up to the nearest day.

3. Allow X days for queue time.

4. Release work to stockroom one week prior to first operation.

Scheduling with a regular calendar is extremely awkward. For example, if a job was to be completed on August 31 (see Figure A-10) and the last operation—inspection—was scheduled to take two days, the previous operation would have to be completed on August 27, not August 29 (Sunday) or August 28 (Saturday). The scheduler would have to reference the calendar continuously to avoid scheduling work on weekends, holidays, during plant vacation shutdown week, etc. Figure A-11 shows a "shop calendar" where only the working days are numbered. This allows the scheduler to do simple arithmetic like "subtract two days from day 412"; thus the previous operation is to be completed on day 410.

			AUGUST			
S	**M**	**T**	**W**	**T**	**F**	**S**
1	2	3	4	5	6	7
8	9	10	11	12	13	14
15	16	17	18	19	20	21
22	23	24	25	26	27	28
29	30	31				

Calendar

Figure A-10 Calendar

Calendar

AUGUST

S	M	T	W	T	F	S
1	2 391	3 392	4 393	5 394	6 395	7
8	9 396	10 397	11 398	12 399	13 400	14
15	16 401	17 402	18 403	19 404	20 405	21
22	23 406	24 407	25 408	26 409	27 410	28
29	30 411	31 412				

Figure A-11 Calendar

Shop calendars are in very common use in manufacturing companies today, but they do have drawbacks. People don't relate to these calendars as easily as they do to a regular calendar. And, of course, they are awkward in dealing with customers who don't use the same shop calendar. Therefore, the shop calendar dates must, once again, be translated back to regular calendar dates. There is a simple solution to this problem with today's computers. A shop calendar can be put in the computer and the computer can do the scheduling using the shop calendar, but print the schedule dates out in regular calendar days. If a company has a shop calendar, there is no reason to discontinue using it if people are used to it. On the other hand, there is no need to introduce the shop calendar today when the computer can do the conversion.

Figure A-12 shows a shop order for the locater pin. This will be used as an example of operations scheduling and, in this example, a shop calendar *will* be used in order to make the arithmetic of scheduling clear. The due date is day 412 and that is determined, in the case of the locater pin that goes into the crankcase half-left, from the material requirements plan.

Operations scheduling works back from this need date to put scheduled finish dates on each operation using scheduling rules like those discussed above. Inspection will be allowed two days. Thus, finish turn must be completed on day 410. It is assumed that the work center file indicates that there are two shifts working in work center 1204 (two shifts at 8 hours apiece equals 16 hours); thus the 27.3 hours required for finish turn will take two days. Planned queue time in this example is assumed to be two days ahead of finish turn. Rough turn must be completed four days earlier than the finish turn must be completed, and its scheduled finish date, therefore, is day 406. The standard hours are calculated by multiplying the quantity by the time per piece and, in this case, adding in the setup time. Where machine operators do not set up their own machines, it might make sense to keep this separate.

It is important to recognize that Figure A-12 shows the information that would be in the computer. *The finish dates would not appear on the shop paperwork that was released to the factory.* The reason is that material requirements planning would be constantly reviewing the need date to see if it had changed. If, for example, the left crankcase halves are scrapped because of a problem with the castings, and the best possible date to have a new lot of castings for the crankcase halves is day 422, the master

Shop Order NN. 18447
Part No. 80021 — Locater Pin
Quant. 500   **Due: 412**   **Release 395**

Oper.	Dept.	Work Center	Desc.	Setup	Per Piece	Std. Hrs.	Finish
10	08	1322	Cut Off	.5	.010	5.5	402
20	32	1600	Rough Turn	1.5	.030	16.5	406
30	32	1204	Finish Turn	3.3	.048	27.3	410
40	11		Inspect				412

Figure A-12 Shop Order NN. 18447

schedule would be changed to indicate that. The shop order for the locater pins in the computer would be given a new finish date of 422 and operation 30 would then become 420, operation 20 would become 416, etc.

Capacity requirements will not be posted against the work centers using the routine shown in Figure A-9. A capacity plan, as shown in Figure A-13, will be the result.

This capacity plan has, of course, been cut apart to show it in the figure. It would include many more shop orders, as well as the planned order releases from MRP, in reality. The locater pins are shown here as a released shop order. (Note: there is no released shop order for locater pins in Figure A-8. It would show as a "scheduled receipt" if there were.) One of the great values of MRP is the fact that it projects "planned order releases." These planned order releases are used to:

1. Generate lower level material requirements.
2. Generate capacity requirements.
3. Determine when lower level material—both purchased and manufactured—must be rescheduled to earlier or later dates.

This ability to see capacity requirements ahead of time is especially important to good manpower planning. Seeing the capacity requirements coming rather than seeing the backlogs of

			Work Center	1600						
Part No.	SO No.	Qty.	Week 396–400	Week 401–405	Week 406–410	Week 411–415	Week 416–420			
91762	17621	50		3.5						
80021	18447	500			16.5					
								Includes Planned Orders		0
Total Std. Hrs.			294	201	345	210	286			

Figure A-13 Capacity Requirements Plan

work out on the factory floor enables factory supervision to do a far better job of leveling production, resulting in less overtime, and less need to hire and lay off people on a short-term basis.

Figure A-14 shows a summary of the capacity requirements over an eight-week period. In practice, this would typically be projected over a far longer period. The summary is drawn from the capacity requirements plan illustrated in Figure A-13 which would also extend much further into the future than the five weeks shown. A typical manpower plan would extend three to six months into the future and would be calculated weekly. A "facilities plan" that would be used for determining what new machine tools were needed would be calculated typically once every two to three months and extended three to four years into the future because of the lead time for procuring machine tools.

The most important information for a foreman is the average hours that he must plan to turn out. This production rate is usually calculated as a four-week average because the individual weekly hours are not particularly significant. The variations between these hours are more random than real. Figure A-13 shows one reason why this happens. The 16.5 hours for part number 80021, the locator pin, are shown in the week bracketed by days 406 to 410. Referring back to Figure A-12, it can be seen that these 16.5 hours are *actually going to be in work center 1600 Tuesday of the previous week!*

Many people have tried to develop elaborate computer load

**Capacity Requirements
Summary (in Standard Hours)**

Week	4-Week Total	4-Week Average	Hours	Week	4-Week Total	4-Week Average	Hours
1	294			5	286		
2	201			6	250		
3	345			7	315		
4	210	1050	263	8	257	1108	277

Figure A-14 Capacity Requirements Summary (in Standard Hours) leveling systems because they were alarmed by the weekly variation in the apparent "load" shown in the capacity requirements plan. These variations are random. They are exaggerated by the fact that capacity plans are usually done in weekly time periods, and any foreman can attest to the fact that the hours never materialize exactly the same way they are shown on the plan. The most important thing to know is the average rate of output required so that *manpower* can be planned accordingly.

In Figure A-14, the four-week averages are 263 standard hours for the first four weeks and 277 for the second four weeks, or an average of 270 standard hours per week. Now the capacity planner must determine whether that capacity requirement can be met. The first step is to find out what the output from the work center has been over the last few weeks. This is called "demonstrated capacity." (This term was coined by David Garwood and is very useful in describing the present capacity of a work center as opposed to its potential capacity when all shifts are manned, etc.)

It is the job of the capacity planner to then determine whether or not the current capacity is sufficient. Or, what needs to be done to get the capacity to meet the plan. Or—as a last resort—to feed back information that the plan cannot be met.

If the plan cannot be met, the master schedule and, perhaps, even the production plans will have to be changed. If, for example, a company has one broach and it is the only one of its type available because it was made specifically for this company, it could well become a bottleneck. If the capacity plan indicates that more hours were required at the broach than could possibly be produced, the master schedule would have to be changed to reflect this.

Once again, however, it's important to emphasize that this is the *last resort.* The job of the capacity planner is to get the capacity that is needed to meet the plan. And that is an important point to emphasize. If there is any problem that exists in practice with capacity planning, it is the fact that people expect the computer to do the capacity planning rather than recognizing that all it can do is generate numbers that will be given to an intelligent, experienced person—the capacity planner—to use in working with other people to fix capacity problems.

Once it is agreed that the capacity requirements can be met, an output control report as shown in Figure A-15 is set up. Three weeks have passed since the one in the figure was made, and the actual standard hours produced (shown in the second line of the figure) are falling far short of the required standard hours at work center 1600. The deviation in the first week was 20 hours. In the second week, it was 50 hours—for a cumulative deviation of 70 hours. In the third week, it was 80 hours, giving a total cumulative deviation of 150 hours. This is a true *control* report with a plan and feedback to show where actual output in standard hours compares with the plan. It shows the deviation from the plan. The 150 hour deviation in week three indicates that 150 standard hours of work required to produce material to meet the master schedule has not been completed.

The amount of tolerance around the plan has to be established. If it were determined, for example, that the company could tolerate being one half week behind schedule, the tolerance in Figure A-15 would be 135 standard hours. When the deviation exceeds 135 standard hours, that would require immediate attention to increase output through overtime, adding people, etc. Whenever the planned rate in the output control report is changed, the deviation will be reset to 0.

It's a good idea to show input to a work center as well as output. That way, when a work center is behind on output because a feeding work center has not given them the work, it can be de-

Output Control
Work Center 1600
Week No. 4
(in Std. Hrs.)

	Week 1	Week 2	Week 3	Week 4
Planned	270	270	270	270
Actual Std.	250	220	190	
Deviation	-20	-70	-150	

Today

Figure A-15 Output Control

tected very quickly since the input report will show the actual input below the planned input. This is called an "input/output report."

The capacity planning and output control reports are concerned with capacity. The dispatch list shown in Figure A-16 is concerned with priority.

The dispatch list is generated daily—or as required—and goes out to the shop floor at the beginning of the day. It shows the sequence in which the jobs are to be run according to the scheduled date for the operation in that work center. The movement of jobs from work center to work center is put in to the computer so that each morning the foremen can have an up-to-date schedule that is driven by MRP. If part 80021 had been rescheduled to a new completion date of day 422 as discussed above, its priority would drop on the dispatch list because its scheduled date would now be 416. This would allow part number 44318 to be made earlier. The dispatch list gives the foremen the priority of jobs so that they can pick the proper job to start next. Since the dispatch list is driven by MRP, it tells the foremen the right sequence in which to run the jobs to do the best job of preventing predicted shortages.

Dispatch List
Work Center No. 1600

Shop Order No.	Part No.	Qty.	Scheduled Date	Std. Hours
17621	91762	50	401	3.5
18430	98340	500	405	19.2
18707	78212	1100	405	28.6
18447	80021	500	406	16.5
19712	44318	120	409	8.4
			Total Hours	76.2

Day 405

Figure A-16 Dispatch List

Section 4
The MRP II Output Reports

The figures thus far in this appendix represent the major operating reports that are used in an MRP II system. Referring back to Figure A-1, the functions of the production plan (Figure A-2), the master schedule (Figure A-6), the material requirements plan (Figures A-7 and A-8), and the capacity requirements plan (Figure A-13) are illustrated. The output control report (Figure A-15) is the means for monitoring output against the plan to be sure that capacity plans are being executed. The dispatch list (Figure A-16) is the report for the factory to use in executing the material plans. Vendor scheduling is the way the material requirements plans are executed with the "outside factories."

It is important to emphasize the feedback functions in a closed loop system. For example, if vendors are not going to ship on time, they must send in an anticipated delay report as soon as they recognize that they have a problem. In the past, ship dates were not valid. The typical company had many past due purchase orders with the vendor. With MRP II—if it is properly managed—dates will represent real need dates, and, thus, it is important to feed back information as quickly as possible to indicate when these dates cannot be met. This, of course, is also true for the factory, where the anticipated delay report should be a regular part of their feedback to the closed loop system.

The financial reports that can be a by-product of these operating reports in an MRP II system are shown in Figure A-17.

We've already discussed the relationship of the production plan and business plan (see Figures A-1 and A-2). In a company where the production plans are kept current and costed out properly, they should be the basis for the business plan. Actual sales, production, and inventory can be recorded against the production plans and they can be used as *control reports*. The business plan can be kept up to date as production plans are changed. Management can see the financial impact of changes in the production plans on the business plan.

The master schedule, costed out, is the basis for *"transfers to*

Operations	Finance
Production Plans	Business Plan
Master Schedules	Shipping budget (make-to-stock companies), transfers to inventory (make-to-stock companies)
Material Requirements Plans	Current inventories, projected consumption, purchase commitments, manufacturing schedules, and projected future inventory balances
Capacity Requirements Plans Input/Output Reports	Labor requirements by labor grade Standard hours of output by work center in units and dollars
Dispatch Lists	Work in process, labor reporting, efficiency reports
Vendor Schedules	Commitments by vendor

Figure A-17 Financial Reports

inventory" in a make-to-stock company or the *shipping budget* in a make-to-order company. This is, of course, the same as "production" in the production plan. Management can review the projected shipping budgets to make sure that the objectives of shipping to budget and shipping the *right* orders to the *right* customers are being properly reconciled.

Figure A-18 shows the inventory of components for a company making pumps. The inventory file is coded to show which components go into the pumps. The first column in the projected available balance shows the on-hand inventory in units extended by the cost. This is the current number of dollars of pump components in inventory. Projected gross requirements from MRP are costed out, as are scheduled receipts. The projected available balance shows the projected future stockroom inventory month by month based on the projected gross requirements derived from the master schedule which, in turn, is derived from the production plan and, in an MRP II system, represents the detailed execution of the business plan.

Costing out the material requirements plan and summarizing it by product group categories results in:

1. On-hand inventory (in dollars) by product group.

2. How much material will be consumed (in dollars) to support the current production plans ("requirements").

Pump Component Inventory — In $(000)

		Month			
		1	2	3	4
Projected Gross Requirements		250	250	300	300
Scheduled Receipts		250	250	270	290
Proj. Avail. Bal.	540	540	540	510	500

Figure A-18

3. What will have to be purchased to support the current production plans (in dollars).

4. What the projected stockroom inventory balances by product group in dollars should be for months into the future.

5. What will have to be made—this is the shop schedule that will become input to capacity planning and can be converted into labor dollars.

Comparing the actual withdrawals from stock against "requirements," the actual purchases against the plan, and the actual inventory dollars against the projected balances, tells management if the plans are really being executed—and if the *business plan* is actually being executed at the detail level.

From a manufacturing point of view, the output of material requirements planning is released shop orders and planned order releases—the shop schedule. When this is run through the capacity requirements planning section of an MRP II system, the result is the standard hours by work center, by time period, required to satisfy the master schedule and the production plans. This can be converted to labor dollars by labor grade, by time period, and by product group. From this information, management can see how many dollars of material and labor will have to be purchased by time period to support any given production plan with its particular product mix. Some companies, in order to project cash flow with greater accuracy, actually offset the due dates by the payable dates.

Costing out the open shop order file that is used to make the dispatch list yields current work in process in dollars. Labor reporting is usually tied in with dispatching and is the basis for labor efficiency reports. The vendor schedules costed out tell how much of the purchased material is due to be shipped *by vendor* by time period to support the plan.

Perhaps, the most important result of an operating system that can work is inventory valuation. When the inventory records are correct—as they have to be for an MRP system to operate—having accounting cost these records out to get the value of the inventory is a very straightforward matter.

When the operating system works, using it to drive the accounting system means that accounting has better numbers to work with than ever before. It also means that the operating system makes more sense to management than ever before because dollars are the language of business. And when the operating system and the financial system are saying the same things, the financial people and the operating people can talk the same language to management rather than presenting conflicting information.

(Note: Material in Appendix A is taken from *Manufacturing Resource Planning: MRP II—Unlocking America's Productivity Potential* by Oliver Wight, Oliver Wight Limited Publications, Inc., 1984)

Appendix B
Survey Results

Background

In 1985, a survey was taken of over one hundred Class A and B users of MRP II (see Appendix C for a definition of Class A, B, C, and D), focusing on the results they had obtained in the area of purchasing. The respondents were primarily purchasing professionals, MRP II project leaders, and production and inventory control managers. This appendix is a summary of the findings of that survey.

The businesses studied represent many different industries. The products they make include: floor sweepers, equipment for the telecommunications industry, cosmetics, pumps, diesel engines, hand tools, valves, forgings, pipe, wood kitchen cabinets, machine tools, instrumentation, trenchers, backhoes, power tools, office furniture, clothing, electronic instruments, cathode ray tubes, autoclaves, chemical processing equipment, photocopiers, ball bearings, fabricated parts, process chemicals, and both high-volume and low-volume parts.

These companies also represent many different types of manufacturing, including make-to-order, make-to-stock, assemble-to-order, and design-to-order. Many of the companies surveyed were leaders in their respective industries; all are located in North America.

The sizes of the companies surveyed varied widely. Their annual volume of purchases ranged from a low of $4 million to over $1 billion. Eighty percent of them purchased less than $30 million worth of goods annually.

Results

Organization

Fifty-five percent of the companies surveyed have one or more persons in the role of vendor scheduler—in other words, someone other than the buyer who schedules the vendors. Thirty percent of the companies have buyer/planners—one person who does the MRP planning, the vendor scheduling, and the buying. Fifteen percent still cling to the traditional "requisition" form of scheduling, in which a material planner writes out a requisition based upon the MRP output and the buyer converts it into a hard-copy purchase order.

Schedules

Of those respondents who did some form of vendor scheduling, 78 percent used a vendor schedule while 22 percent simply gave their computer-generated MRP output sheets directly to the vendors.

Interestingly, three companies reported some form of computer-to-computer linkage (electronic data interchange) with their vendors. One of those companies has placed CRTs in the offices of its key vendors, allowing them to look directly into the company's MRP system at the requirements and orders.

Reporting Structure

The respondents were split neatly down the middle on the reporting structure of the vendor scheduling organization. In almost 50 percent of the companies, the vendor schedulers report to purchasing, and in the other nearly 50 percent, they report to production and inventory control. There was only one exception to the 50-50 split. In that company, the vendor scheduling group reports directly to the materials manager, who is on an equal level with managers of the purchasing department and production and inventory control.

Vendor Scheduler/Buyer Ratio

While the number of parts per buyer or per vendor scheduler varied widely from case to case, the average company surveyed reported one vendor scheduler as being able to support two buyers.

Benefits Achieved

The benefits achieved in the Class A/B MRP II users' purchasing departments are impressive. The survey was designed to quantify benefits in four areas: on-time delivery, lead time reduction, inventory reduction, and purchase cost reduction. Respondents also commented on other areas of benefit, but these comments have not been quantified in any way.

On-Time Delivery

The keys to success in this area can be boiled down to a vendor schedule with valid need dates and intensive vendor education. On-time delivery was measured by comparing due dates with actual delivery dates. Companies using vendor schedules and vendor schedulers averaged an on-time vendor performance level of 97 percent.

A few of the surveyed companies gave their MRP output directly to the vendors. Those companies averaged 93 percent on-time service from their vendors. We theorize that the 4 percent difference may be due to a small amount of misunderstanding by the vendors' personnel on how to interpret the MRP reports.

Those companies that continue to use hard-copy purchase orders averaged on-time vendor delivery performance of only 76 percent. Apparently from the vendors' viewpoint, where traditional purchase orders are used, there is not a great difference between their customers' old systems and MRP II. Therefore, vendor performance does not improve significantly until their customers change to vendor scheduling.

The typical respondent stated 30 to 40 percent of the open purchase orders were past due prior to MRP II implementation. That figure was reduced to between 15 and 20 percent after one month of MRP II because purchasing "rescheduled-out" all the past due orders that weren't needed yet. Five months later, through a combination of vendor education and valid schedules, the level of past due orders was reduced to 3 percent.

Another way to look at vendor delivery performance is in terms of items short in any one week. Users typically cut purchased item shortages from 30 to 50 parts in a week to 4 or 5. As one buyer stated: "We cut the anticipated delay report from two pages to less than half a page, and we know about all those shortages in advance from our vendors." Many companies also commented that particular commodities which had been troublesome before were no longer problems.

Lead Time Reduction

Most companies surveyed saw a dramatic decrease in lead times. Many stated they had no lead times greater than eight weeks. One design-to-order company that is buying capacity from its sand casting vendor has cut the lead time from 26 weeks to eight weeks and eliminated shortages. They forecast capacity requirements to their vendors at the eight-week window but show the actual configuration one week out, when the vendor is actually packing the sand in the mold box.

Inventory Reduction

The surveyed companies also reported significant inventory reductions made possible by MRP II. One company was able to cut its on-hand steel inventory from 13 weeks to five days, while simultaneously eliminating steel shortages. Another turned purchased item inventory 37 times a year, while a clothing manufacturer increased inventory turns on their purchased yarn from 50 to 125 turns. Responses of eight or more inventory turns per year on purchased items were very common.

Purchase Cost Reduction

Companies with a vendor schedule and a vendor scheduler saw an average 11 percent annual reduction in the cost of purchased material. Those with a buyer/planner saw an average 7 percent annual cost reduction. We theorize that the difference in benefits is the result of the time the buyer/planner has to devote to material requirements planning and scheduling. Those companies still using hard-copy purchase orders saw a 2 percent annual cost reduction.

Comments

In general, the respondents were very positive about the use of MRP II and purchasing. Overwhelmingly, they reported they had better information and greater control over their departments than ever before. They knew exactly what was going to be built weekly on every product the company manufactured (through the master production schedule) and what the requirements were on every item they purchased (through MRP).

The only negative MRP II comments uncovered in the survey involved "nervousness" in the master production schedule. Several purchasing managers noted a stable master schedule is critical to purchasing and that their companies sometimes violated the established master schedule policies and time fences. However, all agreed that if the master schedule policies were followed, and all changes inside the firm time fences were reviewed with purchasing first, this nervousness would be minimized.

One purchasing manager summed up the differences MRP II has made in his work life by saying: "If I know what I need to support manufacturing, I have a reasonable chance to get it. Before, I never knew, so we were always fire-fighting. I would never work for another company that didn't have an MRP II system."

Conclusions

The results achieved in each of the four areas studied did not vary with the size or purchasing power of the company. Therefore, the effectiveness of vendor scheduling does not appear to be dependent upon "clout." We believe firmly that it's a function of the desire and the understanding of the people in the purchasing department.

One additional conclusion drawn from this study is that companies that stay with the traditional way of purchasing (hard-copy purchase orders) do not increase their on-time delivery performance dramatically and see little or no cost reduction.

Overall, the benefits of effective vendor scheduling include:

- Improved credibility with the plant and vendors because everyone is working to the same set of numbers.

- Reduced inventory without reducing service to the plant. The right items can be brought in as needed.

- The ability to get planning data to the suppliers. The vendor schedule tells the vendor everything the customer knows about future requirements, both short term and out beyond the vendor's quoted lead time.

- Ninety-five percent or better on-time vendor delivery performance.

- Buyers who can now spend time on value analysis, negotiation, and vendor problems, not expediting.

- Reduced floor expediting because foremen have the correct items when they need them.

- Reduced vendor lead times.

- A more motivated, professional purchasing department.

Appendix C
The ABCD Checklist

The ABCD Checklist is for companies that are currently *operating* MRP systems and want to measure their effectiveness.

A *Class* A MRP user is one that uses MRP in a closed loop mode. They have material requirements planning, capacity planning and control, shop floor dispatching, and vendor scheduling systems in place and being used.

And management uses the system to run the business. They participate in production planning. They sign off on the production plans. They constantly monitor performance on inventory record accuracy, bill of material accuracy, routing accuracy, attainment of the master schedule, attainment of the capacity plans, etc.

In a Class A company, the MRP system provides the game plan that sales, finance, manufacturing, purchasing, and engineering people all work to. They *use* the formal system. The foremen and the purchasing people work to the schedules. There is no shortage list to override the schedules and answer the question, "What material is really needed when?"—that answer comes from the formal MRP system.

Companies using MRP II have gone even a step beyond Class A. They have tied in the financial system and developed simulation capabilities so that the "what if" questions can be answered using the system. In this type of company, management can work with one set of numbers to run the business because the operating system and the financial system use the same numbers.

Technically, then, an MRP II system has the financial and operating systems married together and has a simulation capability. But, the important point is that the system is used as a company game plan. This is what really makes a company Class A.

A *Class B* company has material requirements planning and usually capacity requirements planning and shop floor control systems in place. The Class B user typically hasn't done much with purchasing yet and differs from the Class A user primarily because top management doesn't really use the system to run the business directly. Instead, Class B users see MRP as a production and inventory control system. Because of this, it's easy for a Class B user to become a Class C user very quickly. Another characteristic of the Class B company is that they do *some* scheduling in the shop using MRP, but their shortage list is what really tells them what to make. Class B users typically see most of their benefits from MRP in inventory reduction and improved customer service because they do have more of the right things going through production. Because they haven't succeeded in getting the expediting "monkey" off the backs of the purchasing people and foremen, they haven't seen substantial benefits in reduced purchase costs or improved productivity—and they still have more inventory than they really need.

A *Class C* company uses MRP primarily as an inventory ordering technique rather than as a scheduling technique. Shop scheduling is still being done from the shortage list, and the master schedule in a Class C company is typically overstated. They have not really closed the loop. They probably will get some benefits in inventory reduction as a result of MRP.

A *Class D* company only has MRP really working in the data processing department. Typically, their inventory records are poor. If they have a defined master schedule, it's usually grossly overstated and mismanaged, and little or no results have come from the installation of the MRP system. Ironically, except for the education costs, a Class D company will have spent almost as much as a Class A company. They will have spent about 80% of the total, but not achieved the results.

How to Use the Checklist

Go through the checklist, and try to honestly evaluate where your company stands. This should involve at least two or three people, and there are some instances where partial credit would be ap-

The ABCD Checklist

Technical

YES   NO

1. Time periods for master production scheduling and Material Requirements Planning are weeks or smaller. —   —
2. Master production scheduling and Material Requirements Planning run weekly or more frequently. —   —
3. System includes firm planned order and pegging capability. —   —
4. The master production schedule is visibly managed, not automatic. —   —
5. System includes capacity requirements planning. —   —
6. System includes daily dispatch list. —   —
7. System includes input/output control. —   —

Data Integrity

8. Inventory record accuracy 95% or better. —   —
9. Bill of material accuracy 98% or better. —   —
10. Routing accuracy 95% or better. —   —

Education

11. Initial education of at least 80% of all employees. —   —
12. An ongoing education program. —   —

Use of the System

13. The shortage list has been eliminated. —   —
14. Vendor delivery performance is 95% or better. —   —
15. Vendor scheduling is done out beyond the quoted lead times. —   —
16. Shop delivery performance is 95% or better. —   —
17. Master schedule performance is 95% or better. —   —
18. There are regular (at least monthly) production planning meetings with the general manager and his staff including manufacturing, production and inventory control, engineering, marketing, finance. —   —
19. There is a written master scheduling policy which is adhered to. —   —
20. The system is used for scheduling as well as ordering. —   —
21. MRP is well understood by key people in manufacturing, marketing, engineering, finance, and top management. —   —
22. Management really uses MRP to manage. —   —
23. Engineering changes are effectively implemented. —   —
24. Simultaneous improvement has been achieved in at least two of the following three areas: inventory, productivity, customer service. —   —
25. Operating system is used for financial planning. —   —

A Class A user would be one where the company rated 90 points or higher on the checklist. From 70 to 90 makes a company a Class B user; from 50 to 70, a Class C user; and below 50, a Class D user.

Each company has to use this as a guide in evaluating themselves. If, for example, a company doesn't have any real manu-

propriate. Question 3, for example, could have half credit (two points since the questions each rate four points). Question 21 is another one that could generate partial credit.

facturing, but only purchases and assembles, then questions 5 and 6 would not apply, and full credit would be given even though the company doesn't have capacity planning and a daily dispatch list.

When the weakest areas in the company are identified, then the important issue is to fix the problems. And the problems always come back to people, and their understanding at one level or another. For example, if inventory record accuracy isn't good, that may be because the stockroom people don't understand. It may be because their supervisor doesn't understand, or it may be because the plant manager to whom the stockroom reports doesn't hold people accountable for inventory record accuracy because the plant manager doesn't understand. Understanding is a case of education, and management conveying a message to people about running a business more professionally.

(Note: Appendix C is taken from *Manufacturing Resource Planning: MRP II—Unlocking America's Productivity Potential* by Oliver Wight, Oliver Wight Limited Publications, Inc., 1984.)

Appendix D
The Implementation Plan

MRP II Detailed Implementation Plan

More and more people are asking for information on the implementation and operation of MRP systems. These people are not interested in being sold on MRP. MRP systems work. The proof is available and companies are using them every day. People who understand the fundamentals and the logical simplicity of MRP are looking for a proven way to implement the system.

This detailed implementation plan is a road map to help people implement MRP systems. The implementation plan outlines the basic functional areas needed to implement MRP. These functional areas are then broken down into specific milestones. This listing of broad functional areas and specific tasks provides a very practical plan.

People Using MRP

The implementation plan is also meant for companies using an MRP system. There are many companies which have the technical part of an MRP system in place. Yet, they are not using the system well. The implementation plan can help these companies. The jobs in improving an MRP system are the same as the jobs to implement it correctly. The only difference is that some of these jobs may have already been done. If so, they can be deleted from the plan.

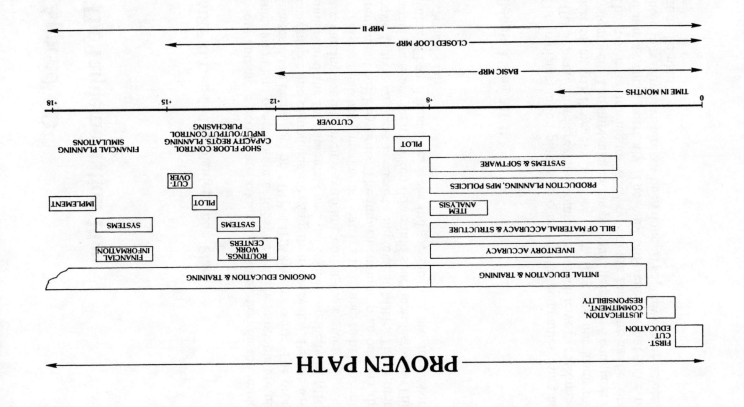

PROVEN PATH

TIME IN MONTHS

| | +8 | +12 | +15 | +18 |

MRP II

CLOSED LOOP MRP

BASIC MRP

CUTOVER

PILOT

SYSTEMS & SOFTWARE

PRODUCTION PLANNING, MPS POLICIES

FINANCIAL PLANNING
SIMULATIONS

SHOP FLOOR CONTROL
CAPACITY REQTS. PLANNING
INPUT/OUTPUT CONTROL
PURCHASING

CUT-OVER

PILOT

IMPLEMENT

ITEM ANALYSIS

SYSTEMS

SYSTEMS

BILL OF MATERIAL ACCURACY & STRUCTURE

FINANCIAL INFORMATION

ROUTINGS, WORK CENTERS

INVENTORY ACCURACY

ONGOING EDUCATION & TRAINING

INITIAL EDUCATION & TRAINING

JUSTIFICATION, COMMITMENT, RESPONSIBILITY

FIRST-CUT EDUCATION

Using the Plan

The implementation plan is a generalized framework applicable to nearly any company. Its two primary uses are:

1. To provide a clear statement of priorities—to separate the vital and trivial, and keep them in perspective.

2. To provide a road map for implementation.

The implementation plan is organized to constantly focus attention on the items that have the greatest impact on the potential for success. The people part of an MRP system is fully 80% of the system. The system will only work when people understand what it is, how it works, and what their responsibilities are. For this reason, the education and training are listed at the front of the implementation plan. The computer software and programming effort is not as likely to be something which prevents the success of an MRP system, and so this topic is covered later in the plan.

The other purpose is to provide a detailed schedule of events that have to be accomplished in order to implement the system. The most effective way to use the plan is to tailor the plan to each company and then use it as the agenda for management reviews of implementation progress.

Practicality

This implementation plan is not a theoretical exercise. In the six years since the first version of the plan was developed, it has been used successfully by a number of companies. Whether these companies would have been successful without the plan, I cannot say. But it does work, it is practical, and those who have used it swear by it.

Tailoring the Plan to Your Company

The implementation plan is a general framework stated in terms of departments and job titles. The departments and job titles should be replaced by the names of the people within the organization who will be responsible for the tasks.

The implementation plan also contains an approximate time frame for scheduling the tasks under each of the functional topics. The scheduled due dates for the tasks in implementation are given under the heading "DATE." These due dates were developed based on the dependence of some tasks on others. The times on the plan, +3 and +7 for example, are months relative to a starting point. A time of +3 means the task should be completed three months after the start date. The start date used in the plan is the date that formal commitment is given to the project.

The plan should be rewritten to include calendar dates in place of the scheduled completion dates in months. Columns should also be added for the scheduled start date, the actual start date, and the actual completion date. The scheduled start dates are not on the generalized plan since the size of the different tasks will vary from company to company. The actual start and actual completion dates should be included on the plan to indicate the progress or lack of it during the management reviews of implementation.

The comments column on the implementation plan is meant to give a short explanation of the phases of the plan and tasks that make up each phase. Some people choose to leave these explanations in the final version of the plan, others leave them out. In either case, additional comments on the progress of the tasks should also be included as the plan is periodically updated. These comments would indicate, for example, the results of the cycle counts, or any other information about one of the items in the plan.

A company may also have to add or delete tasks from the implementation plan to account for situations that are a part of the implementation, or work that has already been done. As an example of an item that would be deleted from the plan, a company may have already enclosed the stockrooms and may have started cycle counting. In this case, it makes no sense to count 100 parts as a starting point. As an example of an item that would have to be added to the plan, a company may have to convert to a different computer to do MRP. In this case, the conversion from one computer to the other should be included on the detailed implementation plan.

Figure D-1 is an example of the implementation plan before and after it has been tailored to a company. This example includes replacement of departments and job titles with people's names, the inclusion of calendar dates with columns for scheduling dates, and some comments on tasks that are working.

MRP DETAILED IMPLEMENTATION PLAN

TASK		RESPONSIBLE	DATE	COMMENTS
A.	Measure 100 parts as a starting point.	Stockroom Mgr.	+1	This will help assess the work that needs to be done to bring the inventory records to 95%.
B.	Map out limited access to the stockroom areas.	Stockroom Mgr.	+1.	Lay out any stockroom changes that are necessary to insure limited access.
C.	Provide the tools for limited access and transaction recording.	Top Management Stockroom Mgr. Team Leader DP Mgr.	+3	A fence, enough stockroom people, adequate space, counting scales, transaction forms, labels, skids, etc.

TASK		RESPONSIBLE	— SCHEDULED —		— ACTUAL —	
			START	DUE	START	DUE
A.	Measure 100 parts as a starting point.	R. Ferris	6/20/80	6/27/80	6/20/80	6/24/80
	Results indicate that the inventory accuracy is 63%.					
B.	Map out limited access to the stockroom areas.	R. Ferris K. Miller	6/1/80	7/1/80	6/5/80	
	Lay out any stockroom changes that are necessary to insure limited access. Main and spare parts stockrooms to be enclosed and third stockroom to be consolidated into the existing stockrooms.					
C.	Provide the tools for limited access and transaction recording.	D. Roser R. Ferris K. Miller H. Arner	7/15/80	9/1/80		
	A fence, enough stockroom people, adequate space, counting scales, transaction forms, labels, skids, etc.					

Figure D-1

MRP DETAILED IMPLEMENTATION PLAN

TASK	RESPONSIBLE	DATE	COMMENTS
1. **First-cut education.**	Top Management P&IC Shop Management	−1	What is MRP and how does it work? Why should we, as a company, commit to it? The courses should be the equivalent of the following courses offered by The Oliver Wight Companies P.O. Box 435 Newbury, New Hampshire 03255 (800) 258-3862 or (603) 763-5926
	Top Management P&IC Shop Management		MRP II: Manufacturing Resource Planning For Top Management MRP II: Manufacturing Resource Planning - 5 Day
2. **Justification, commitment, and assignment of responsibility.**	Top Management P&IC	0	Formal commitment to the project.
A. Prepare justification.	P&IC Shop Management	0	Cost/Benefit.
B. Commit to the project.	Top Management	0	
C. Set up implementation team and team leader.	Top Management	0	Implementation team leader is full-time. His responsibility is to make the MRP system work by coordinating and managing the project.
D. Schedule periodic management project reviews.	Top Management	0	Approximately every month. To include all those responsible for parts of the project currently active.
E. Schedule periodic visits from a consultant with experience in implementing successful MRP systems.	Top Management	0	The consultant should have successfully implemented a system or worked with successful systems. Schedule visits from once a month to once every three months.

MRP DETAILED IMPLEMENTATION PLAN

TASK	RESPONSIBLE	DATE	COMMENTS
3. **Detailed education and training.**	Team Leader	0+8	This phase of the plan is aimed at the people part of the system.

> The objective of this part of the plan is to give the people operating the system an understanding of the system and the means to use it effectively. Education and training must translate the general principles of MRP into the specifics of operation at the company.
>
> The plan separates education and training. Education is the broad-based understanding of MRP which is essential. Training is the detailed knowledge of reports, forms, etc.
>
> The education and training are structured in levels. People in the company attend outside courses. These people then serve as teachers and train their own people.

TASK	RESPONSIBLE	DATE	COMMENTS
A. Outside courses for people who will be teachers at the in-house courses.		+1+3	The courses should be the equivalent of the following courses offered by The Oliver Wight Companies P. O. Box 435 Newbury, New Hampshire 03255 (800) 258-3862 or (603) 763-5926
	Team Leader		MRP II: Manufacturing Resource Planning—5-Day
	Steering Committee Chairman		MRP II: Successful Implementation
	P&IC Mgr.		MRP II: Successful Implementation
	Purch. Mgr.		MRP II: Manufacturing Resource Planning—5-Day
	Plant Supt.		MRP II: Manufacturing Resource Planning—5-Day
	Stockroom Mgr.		MRP II: Manufacturing Resource Planning—5-Day
	Engr. Mgr.		MRP II: Manufacturing Resource Planning—5-Day
	Sales/Mktg. Mgr.		MRP II: Manufacturing Resource Planning For Top Management
	DP Mgr.		MRP II: Manufacturing Resource Planning For Top Management
			MRP II: Manufacturing Resource Planning—5-Day

MRP DETAILED IMPLEMENTATION PLAN

TASK	RESPONSIBLE	DATE	COMMENTS
B. Purchase or lease the MRP video courses for in-house education.	Team Leader	+1	These video courses will serve as the framework for all the educational courses in the following educational plan. The current library consists of 53 video tapes, approximately 33 hours of video taped education on MRP. The MRP video library is available through: The Oliver Wight Companies 5 Oliver Wight Drive Essex Junction, Vermont 05452 (802) 878-8161 or (800) 343-0625
C. Teachers course. Video education.	Team Leader	+1½	The team leader and all teachers go through the video courses to translate the general principles of MRP into the specifics of operation at the company. *Attendees:* All teachers. *Length:* Approx. 80 hrs.
D. Top Management Course. Video education.	Team Leader	+2+8	*Attendees:* Pres., all VPs, Plant Superintendent, others as appropriate. *Length:* Approx. 40 hrs.
E. Production and inventory control. Video education.	P&IC Mgr.	+2+8	*Attendees:* All people in P&IC. *Length:* Approx. 80 hrs.
Outside workshop	Master Scheduler	+3	Outside master scheduling workshop for one or more master schedulers. The workshop should be the equivalent of the one offered by The Oliver Wight Companies.

MRP DETAILED IMPLEMENTATION PLAN

TASK	RESPONSIBLE	DATE	COMMENTS
In-house training.	P&IC Mgr.	+7+8	*Attendees:* All people in P&IC. *Coverage:* All forms, reports, and documents that will be used by the people in P&IC. This includes a dry run of the system, sometimes called a "conference room pilot," to gain experience in using the reports and transactions.
F. Purchasing. Video education.	Purch. Mgr.	+2+8	*Attendees:* All people in purchasing. *Length:* Approx. 45 hrs.
Outside workshop.	Purch. Mgr. Buyers	+5	Outside purchasing workshop for one or more buyers. The workshop should be the equivalent of the one offered by The Oliver Wight Companies.
In-house training.	Purch. Mgr.	+7+8	*Attendees:* All people in purchasing. *Coverage:* All forms, reports, and documents that will be used by the people in purchasing. This includes a dry run of the system, sometimes called a "conference room pilot," to gain experience in using the reports and transactions.
G. Shop foreman. Video education.	VP Mfg. Plant Supt.	+2+8	*Attendees:* All shop foremen. *Length:* Approx. 40-45 hrs.
Outside workshop.	Shop Foreman	+5	Outside shop floor control and capacity requirements planning workshop. The workshop would be the equivalent of the one offered by The Oliver Wight Companies.
In-house training.	Plant Supt.	+7+8	*Attendees:* All shop foremen. *Coverage:* All forms, reports, and documents that will be used by the shop people. This includes a dry run using the documents.

MRP DETAILED IMPLEMENTATION PLAN

TASK	RESPONSIBLE	DATE	COMMENTS
H. Stockroom people. Video education.	Stockroom Mgr.	+2+4	*Attendees:* Anyone who will be making inventory transactions. *Length:* Approx. 15 hrs.
Outside workshop.	Stockroom Mgr.	+3	Outside inventory accuracy workshop for one or more stockroom managers. The workshop should be the equivalent of the one offered by The Oliver Wight Companies.
In-house training.	Stockroom Mgr.	+3	*Attendees:* Anyone who will be making inventory transactions. *Coverage;* All forms, reports, and documents that will be used in the inventory transaction system.
I. Sales and marketing. Video education.	Sales/Mktg. Mgr.	+3+8	*Attendees:* All sales and marketing people. This course is usually divided into two courses. One for those people in-house and one for those in district sales offices. *Length:* Approx. 25–30 hrs.
In-house training.	Sales/Mktg. Leader	+8	*Attendees:* All in-house sales and marketing people. *Coverage:* All forms, reports, and documents used in master scheduling and forecasting applicable to the sales and marketing people.

MRP DETAILED IMPLEMENTATION PLAN

TASK	RESPONSIBLE	DATE	COMMENTS
J. Engineering. Video education.	Engr. Mgr.	+2+8	*Attendees:* Anyone who will be working with bills of material or routings. *Length:* Approx. 30–40 hrs.
Outside workshop.	Engr. Mgr.	+3	Outside bill of material structuring workshop for the engineering manager and several of the engineers who will be structuring bills of material. The bill of material workshop should be the equivalent of the material workshop offered by the Oliver Wight Companies.
In-house training.	Engr. Mgr.	+5	*Attendees:* Anyone who will be working with bills of material or routings. *Coverage:* All forms, reports, and documents that will be used to maintain bills of material and routings.
K. Data processing. Video education.	DP Mgr.	+2+8	*Attendees:* Anyone who will be working with the MRP programs or files. *Length:* Approx. 55 hrs.
L. Finance. Video education.	Mgr. Finance/ Accounting	+2+8	*Attendees:* All people in finance. *Length:* Approx. 35 hrs.
Outside workshop.	Mgr. Finance/ Accounting	+2+8	Outside finance and accounting workshop for one or more managers of finance and/or accounting. The workshop should be the equivalent of the one offered by The Oliver Wight Companies.
M. Lead men and setup men.	Shop Foremen	+2+8	*Attendees:* All setup or lead men. *Length:* Approx. 20 hrs.

MRP DETAILED IMPLEMENTATION PLAN

TASK	RESPONSIBLE	DATE	COMMENTS
N. Distribution center managers. Video education.	Distribution Mgr.	+2+8	*Attendees:* All distribution center or branch warehouse managers. *Length:* Approx. 20 hrs.
Outside workshop.	Distribution Mgr. DC Mgrs. Master Scheduler P&IC Mgr.	+3	Outside distribution resource planning workshop for the manager of distribution, one or more distribution center or branch warehouse managers, one or more master schedulers, P&IC manager. The workshop should be the equivalent of the one offered by The Oliver Wight Companies.
O. Distribution center employees. Video education.	DC Mgrs.	+3+8	*Attendees:* All distribution center employees. *Length:* Approx. 15 hrs.
P. Introduction to all direct labor employees.	VP Mfg. Plant Supt.	+3+8	*Attendees:* All direct labor employees. *Length:* Approx. 2 hrs.
Q. Anyone else affected by the system and not covered in the courses above.	Team Leader	+8	*Attendees:* As required. *Length:* As required.
4. Inventory accuracy.	Stockroom Mgr.	+8	This phase of the plan is aimed at bringing the inventory accuracy to 95% of the items within the counting error. This must be accomplished before the pilot program can be started. This includes distribution centers or branch warehouses.
A. Measure 100 parts as a starting point.	Stockroom Mgr.	+1	This will help assess the work that needs to be done to bring the inventory records to 95%.
B. Map out limited access to the stockroom areas.	Stockroom Mgr.	+1	Lay out any stockroom changes that are necessary to insure limited access.

MRP DETAILED IMPLEMENTATION PLAN

TASK	RESPONSIBLE	DATE	COMMENTS
C. Provide the tools for limited access and transaction recording.	Top Management Stockroom Mgr. Team Leader DP Mgr.	+3	A fence, enough stockroom people, adequate space, counting scales, transaction forms, labels, skids, etc.
D. Assign responsibility for the inventory accuracy.	Top Management	+3	The inventory manager and his people are now responsible for the inventory accuracy. Change job descriptions where necessary.
E. Start counting a control group of 100 parts.	Stockroom Mgr.	+3	Control group parts are counted once every ten days. Any inventory errors are investigated to find the cause of the error.
F. Each ten days a report is published showing the results of the control group.	Stockroom Mgr.	+3 on	The report should show the history of the inventory accuracy and the cause of the errors.
G. Start cycle counting all inventory items.	Stockroom Mgr.	+5 on	All parts are counted periodically. A simple method would be to count A and B items twice a year, and the C items once a year.
H. Bring the inventory accuracy to 95% of the parts within counting error.	Stockroom Mgr.	+8	As measured by the results of cycle counting the items in inventory, and not based only on the control group items.
5. **Bill of material accuracy.**	Engr. Mgr. P&IC Mgr.	+8	This phase of the plan is aimed at bringing bill of material accuracy to 98%. The tasks in this phase must be completed before the pilot program can begin. Both design and production engineering should participate in structuring the bills of material.

MRP DETAILED IMPLEMENTATION PLAN

TASK	RESPONSIBLE	DATE	COMMENTS
A. Measure 100 bills of material as a starting point.	Engineering	+3	This will help assess the work that needs to be done to eliminate errors from the bills of material.
B. Decide and assign responsibility for the accuracy of bills of material.	Top Management	+3	This may involve centralizing some responsibilities and setting up procedures to control the flow of documents if these are not already present.
C. Verify the bills of material for correct part numbers and quantities per assembly.	Engineering	+8	This requires either a line-by-line audit or an exception system, like stockroom pulls, to point out bill of material errors. Either method must highlight and correct any errors in component part numbers or quantities per assembly.
D. Verify the bills of material to show the correct structure of the product.	Engineering	+8	This requires restructuring the bills where necessary to show: 1. The way material moves on the shop floor. 2. Raw materials on the bills of material. 3. Modules or self-consumed assemblies where needed.
E. Decide on and implement bill of material policies.	Top Management Engineering P&IC	+5	Policies: 1. Engineering change procedure. 2. Documenting new or special products.
6. Item analysis.	P&IC Mgr.	+8	This phase of the plan covers the verification or assignment of the ordering rules.
A. Measure 100 items as a starting point.	P&IC Purchasing Team Leader	+1	The parts are checked for correct lead times, ordering quantities, and safety stock (if applicable). This measurement will help assess the work that needs to be done.

MRP DETAILED IMPLEMENTATION PLAN

TASK	RESPONSIBLE	DATE	COMMENTS
B. Agree upon and assign responsibility for the ordering rules.	P&IC Purchasing	+2	Responsibilities depend on how purchasing fits into the organization and whether or not the planner/buyer concept is used.
C. Verify or establish ordering policies.	P&IC Purchasing	+8	Decide between fixed order policy or lot-for-lot ordering. Dynamic order policies like part period balancing are not recommended.
D. Verify or establish order quantities and order modifiers.	P&IC Purchasing	+8	Assign order quantities for fixed order policy items. Modifiers should be assigned where they are appropriate.
E. Verify or establish lead times.	P&IC Purchasing	+8	*Manufactured parts:* 1. Use simple scheduling rules. 2. Be consistent. *Purchased parts:* 1. Use current lead times.
F. Verify or establish safety stock levels.	P&IC Purchasing	+8	*Independent demand items:* 1. Consistent with the master schedule policy. *Dependent demand items:* 1. In special circumstances.
7. Master production schedule preparation.	Top Management Marketing P&IC Shop Management	+8	This phase of the plan covers the work required to set up a working master production schedule. Must include resource requirements planning.
A. Develop a production planning function.	Top Management Marketing P&IC Shop Management	+6	Production planning is basic strategic planning to develop a statement of production which is in families of products and by months.

MRP DETAILED IMPLEMENTATION PLAN

TASK	RESPONSIBLE	DATE	COMMENTS
B. Develop a master scheduling function.	P&IC	+6	Master scheduling takes the production plan and translates it into a specific statement of production. The master schedule is a statement of production in specific item numbers and by weeks.
C. Develop a master schedule policy.	Top Management Marketing P&IC Shop Management	+6	The master schedule policy should cover the following points for both production planning and master scheduling: 1. Procedure for changing the production plan or master production schedule. This procedure should include who can request a change, how the proposed change is investigated, and who should approve it before it is implemented. 2. Periodic reviews of the forecast and actual sales, also the master schedule and the actual production. The purpose of these reviews is to determine whether or not the production plan or master production schedule should be changed.
D. Begin operating the production plan and master production schedule.	Top Management Marketing P&IC Shop Management	+8	The first production plan and master production schedule are developed.

MRP DETAILED IMPLEMENTATION PLAN

TASK	RESPONSIBLE	DATE	COMMENTS
8. Systems work and software selection.	DP Mgr.	+8	This phase of the plan outlines the work that needs to be done in selecting software and accomplishing the systems work and programming for the MRP system.
A. Review and select software to be used.	Data Processing P&IC Shop Management	+2	Software should be evaluated using the software evaluations from: The Oliver Wight Companies 5 Oliver Wight Drive Essex Junction, Vermont 05452 (802) 878-8161 or (800) 343-0625
B. Systems work, programming, and testing of inventory transactions.	Data Processing	+5	Issues, receipts, cycle counting.
C. Systems work, programming, and testing of bills of material.	Data Processing	+6	Normal bill of material functions.
D. Systems work, programming, and testing of scheduled receipts.	Data Processing	+6½	Scheduling receipts: 1. Manufacturing orders. 2. Purchase orders. 3. Distribution orders.
E. Systems work, programming, and testing of the MRP logic.	Data Processing	+8	Any modifications that need to be made.
F. Systems work, programming, and testing of the master schedule system.	Data Processing	+8	Master scheduling and production planning support.
G. Agree on time schedules and cutoff times.	Data Processing	+6	Times for reports, transactions and cutoff times for transactions to the system.

MRP DETAILED IMPLEMENTATION PLAN

TASK	RESPONSIBLE	DATE	COMMENTS
9. Pre-installation tasks.	P&IC Mgr. Team Leader	+8	This phase of the plan covers the tasks that immediately precede the pilot program. Must include some form of shop dispatching.
A. Set up planner structure and part responsibilities.	P&IC	+8	Which planners are responsible for which groups of parts? Decide among vertical or horizontal responsibility: 1. Vertical product line-oriented. 2. Horizontal department-oriented.
B. Set up procedures for handling both top down and bottom up closed loop planning.	P&IC Shop Foremen Purchasing	+8	Specific procedures for rescheduling, order release, and feedback of anticipated delays.
C. Physical cleanup.	P&IC Shop Foremen Purchasing	+8	Physical cleanup of the shop floor to insure that each open order has the required component parts, and that all parts on the floor are on an open order. Parts not covered by a shop order should be returned to the stockroom. All manufacturing orders and purchase orders should be verified.
10. Pilot program.	Everyone involved so far	+8+9	This is the pilot program. It is a trial run of the system on one or a group of product lines that total several hundred part numbers. The purpose is to verify that the system is giving correct information.
A. Monitor the critical measurements.	Team Leader	+8+9	Verify that the system is providing correct information and that people are comfortable using the system.

TASK	RESPONSIBLE	DATE	COMMENTS
11. **Cutover.**	Everyone involved so far.	+9+12	This phase of the plan outlines the sequence that is used to move from the pilot program to full implementation on all product lines.
A. Group the remaining product lines into three or four divisions.	P&IC	+9	Divisions should contain product lines that are similar or share common parts.
B. Bring each division onto MRP, one division at a time.	P&IC	+9+12	As each division is put onto MRP, set up planner coverage so the product lines involved get intense planner coverage until they are quieted down.

END OF FIRST MAJOR SECTION IN IMPLEMENTATION

TASK	RESPONSIBLE	DATE	COMMENTS
12. **Training for shop floor control, capacity requirements planning, input/output control, and purchasing.**	Shop Management	+15	This phase of the plan outlines the training for shop floor control, capacity requirements planning and purchasing. This training has the same objectives and the same basic course outline as the MRP training covered previously.
A. Shop Foremen. In-house training.	Plant Supt.	+15	*Attendees:* All shop foremen. *Coverage:* All forms, reports, and documents that will be used in the shop floor control and capacity requirements planning systems.
B. Planners. In-house training.	P&IC Mgr.	+15	*Attendees:* All planners that will be working with the shop people. *Coverage:* All forms, reports, and documents that will be used in the shop floor control and capacity requirements planning systems.

TASK	RESPONSIBLE	DATE	COMMENTS
C. Shop dispatchers. In-house training.	Shop Foremen	+15	*Attendees:* All shop dispatchers. *Coverage:* All forms, reports and documents that will be used in the shop floor control and capacity requirements planning systems.
D. Purchasing. In-house training.	Purch. Mgr.	+15	*Attendees:* All purchasing people. *Coverage:* All forms, reports and documents that will be used in vendor follow-up and vendor negotiation.
13. Routing accuracy.	Shop Foremen Prod. Engr.	+15	This phase of the plan outlines the work that needs to be done to get routing accuracy to 95%.
A. Measure 100 routings as a starting point.	Shop Foremen Prod. Engr.	+10	This will help assess the work that needs to be done to eliminate errors from the routings.
B. Decide on and assign responsibility for the accuracy of the routings.	Top Management	+11	This may involve centralizing some responsibilities or defining areas of responsibilities if these do not already exist.
C. Verify that the routings show the operations correctly.	Shop Foremen Prod. Engr.	+15	This requires either a line-by-line audit of the routing or an exception system to point out routing errors. Either method must highlight and correct the errors in the routings. The routings should be verified for the following: 1. The correct operations and work centers. 2. The correct operation sequence. 3. A reasonable standard that can be used in scheduling.

MRP DETAILED IMPLEMENTATION PLAN

TASK	RESPONSIBLE	DATE	COMMENTS
14. **Work center identification.**	Shop Foremen Prod. Engr.	+15	This phase of the plan outlines the simple steps that are required to define and classify the work centers.
A. Identify work centers.	Shop Foremen Prod. Engr.	+15	Decide which machines or groups of machines will be called work centers. In some cases a single machine will be a work center. In others, a group of similar machines will be a work center.
15. **Systems work.**	DP Mgr.	+15	This phase of the plan outlines the systems work and programming that must be done for shop floor control and capacity requirements planning.
A. Systems work, programming, and testing of shop floor control.	Data Processing	+15	Shop floor control functions.
B. Systems work, programming, and testing of capacity requirements planning.	Data Processing	+15	Capacity requirements planning functions.
C. Systems work, programming, and testing of input/output control.	Data Processing	+15	Input/output control report.
D. Systems work, programming, and testing for purchasing.	Data Processing	+15	Vendor follow-up and vendor negotiation reports.

MRP DETAILED IMPLEMENTATION PLAN

TASK	RESPONSIBLE	DATE	COMMENTS
16. Implementation of shop floor control.	Shop Foremen P&IC	+15 +16	The implementation of shop floor control uses a pilot program since new transactions and disciplines are being used on the shop floor.
A. Implement shop floor control on a pilot group of parts.	Shop Foremen P&IC	+15	The pilot should be large enough to provide one hundred or so shop orders. It is also helpful to use a product line that will create shop orders under shop floor control in all departments.
B. Implement shop floor control on the remaining items.	Shop Foremen P&IC	+15½	Cut over remaining items.
17. Implement capacity requirements planning, input/output control, and purchasing.	Shop Foremen P&IC Purch. Mgr.	+16	This is a simple implementation. Capacity requirements planning, input/output control, and purchasing negotiation reports are simply stated.

END OF SECOND MAJOR SECTION IN IMPLEMENTATION

MRP DETAILED IMPLEMENTATION PLAN

TASK	RESPONSIBLE	DATE	COMMENTS
18. Training for financial planning and simulation.	Mgr. Finance/ Accounting, P&IC Mgr.	+ 18	This phase of the plan outlines the training for financial planning and simulations. This training has the same objectives and the same basic course outline as the MRP training covered previously.
A. Finance and accounting. In-house training.	Mgr. Finance/ Accounting	+ 18	Attendees: People in finance and accounting. Coverage: All forms, reports, and documents that will be used.
B. Production and inventory control. In-house training.	P&IC Mgr.	+ 18	Attendees: People in P&IC. Coverage: Differences between simulations and normal operation of the system.
19. Develop financial planning numbers.	Mgr. Finance/ Accounting	+ 18	These numbers are used to do inventory projections, cash flow projections, and fixed overhead allocations. Numbers include: 1. Cost by item. 2. Labor costs. 3. Machinery operating costs. 4. Fixed overhead allocations by work center, group of work centers, or departments.

TASK	RESPONSIBLE	DATE	COMMENTS
20. **Implement financial planning and simulations.**	Mgr. Finance/ Accounting P&IC Mgr.	+18	No pilot is needed. Begin running the programs and verify the numbers before using for decisions. Types of simulations available include: 1. Changed master production schedule: A. Material impact. B. Capacity impact. C. Financial impact. D. Marketing impact. 2. Make/Buy simulations. 3. Different forecast—same MPS. 4. Sales promotions—same or different MPS. 5. New product introductions.

Darryl Landvater
The Oliver Wight Companies
5 Oliver Wight Drive
Essex Junction, Vermont 05452
(802) 878-8161 or (800) 343-0625

Appendix E
The Oliver Wight Companies' Services

Preparing yourself to implement a Class A MRP II system requires careful study of a huge amount of information, far more than could be included in this or any other book. The Oliver Wight Companies can provide further assistance in getting ready, including books on the subject, live education, videotaped in-plant education, consultation, and reviews of commercially available software packages.

Oliver Wight Limited Publications, Inc.

Oliver Wight Limited Publications, Inc. was created in 1981 to publish books on MRP II, written by leading educators and consultants in the field. Titles include:

Manufacturing Resource Planning: MRP II—Unlocking America's Productivity Potential by the late Oliver W. Wight. Co-published in 1984 with Van Nostrand Reinhold.

The Executive's Guide to Successful MRP II by the late Oliver W. Wight. Co-published in 1981 with Prentice-Hall.

DRP: Distribution Resource Planning—Distribution Management's Most Powerful Tool by Andre J. Martin. Co-published with Prentice-Hall, Inc. in 1983.

Focus Forecasting: Computer Techniques for Inventory Control by Bernard T. Smith. Published in 1984.

MRP II: Making It Happen—The Implementers' Guide to Success with Manufacturing Resource Planning, by Thomas F. Wallace. Published in 1985.

For more information, or to order publications, contact:

Oliver Wight Limited Publications, Inc.
5 Oliver Wight Drive
Essex Junction, VT 05452
800-343-0625 or 802-878-8161

Oliver Wight Education Associates

OWEA is made up of a group of independent MRP II educators and consultants around the world who share a common philosophy and common goals. Classes directed towards both upper- and middle-level management are being taught in various locations around the U.S. and Canada, as well as abroad. For a Detailed Class Brochure, listing course descriptions, instructors, costs, dates, and locations, or for the name of a recommended consultant in your area, please contact:

Oliver Wight Education Associates
P.O. Box 435
Newbury, NH 03255
800-258-3862 or 603-763-5926

Oliver Wight Video Productions, Inc.

The Oliver Wight Video Library offers companies the video-based materials they need to teach the "critical mass" of their employees about the principles of MRP II. The Library is accompanied by Course Guides to assist instructors in directing the discussion sessions that supplement the information on tape. For more information on obtaining the Oliver Wight Video Library, contact:

Oliver Wight Video Productions, Inc.
5 Oliver Wight Drive
Essex Junction, VT 05452
800-343-0625 or 802-878-8161

Oliver Wight Software Research, Inc.

To help you make the right choice about software in a reasonable length of time, Oliver Wight Software Research (formerly known as Manufacturing Software Systems, Inc.) offers Software Evaluations and Audits, comprehensive reviews of the capabilities of many of the most popular packages on the market today. All reviews are based on the MRP II Standard Software System Description, a research document outlining all the functions required to perform Manufacturing Resource Planning. The Standard System is also available for use as an in-house evaluation and teaching aid. OWSR also offers a three-day course entitled, "Systems, Data, and Software Selection," as well as Evaluation Consulting Support, to guide companies through the in-house evaluation process.

For more information, contact:

Oliver Wight Software Research, Inc.
5 Oliver Wight Drive
Essex Junction, VT 05452
800-343-0625 or 802-878-8161

Appendix F
Bibliography

Martin, Andre. *DRP: Distribution Resource Planning—Distribution Management's Most Powerful Tool*. Essex Junction, VT: Oliver Wight Limited Publications, Inc., 1983.

Smith, Bernard T. *Focus Forecasting: Computer Techniques for Inventory Control*. Boston: CBI Publishing Company, Inc., 1978.

Wallace, Thomas F. *MRP II: Making It Happen—The Implementers' Guide to Success with Manufacturing Resource Planning*. Essex Junction, VT: Oliver Wight Limited Publications, Inc., 1985.

Wight, Oliver W. *Manufacturing Resource Planning: MRP II—Unlocking America's Productivity Potential*. Revised Edition. Essex Junction, VT: Oliver Wight Limited Publications, Inc., 1984.

———. *The Executive's Guide to Successful MRP II*. Essex Junction, VT: Oliver Wight Limited Publications, Inc., 1981.

———. *Production and Inventory Management in the Computer Age*. Essex Junction, VT: Oliver Wight Limited Publications, Inc. 1974.

Appendix G
Glossary

Many of the terms found in this glossary have been drawn or adapted from the *APICS Dictionary*, Fifth Edition, 1984, American Production and Inventory Control Society, Inc. The editor of this dictionary is Thomas F. Wallace, and John E. Schorr contributed many of the purchasing-related definitions.

ACKNOWLEDGMENT A communication by a vendor to advise a purchaser that a purchase order has been received. It usually implies acceptance of the order by the vendor.

ACTION MESSAGE An output of an MRP II system that identifies the need for and the type of action to be taken to correct a current or a potential problem. Examples of action messages are "release order," "reschedule out," "cancel," etc.

AGENT A person acting for another who is authorized to perform or transact certain business for the other. In purchasing, the person authorized to purchase goods and services for a company.

ANTICIPATED DELAY REPORT A report, normally issued by both manufacturing and purchasing to the material planning function, regarding jobs or purchase orders which will not be completed on time, why not, and when they will be completed. This is an essential ingredient of a closed loop MRP system. Except perhaps in very large companies, the anticipated delay report is manually prepared.

BILL OF MATERIAL A listing of all the subassemblies, intermediates, parts and raw materials, etc. that go into a parent item, showing the quantity of each component required. May also be called "formula," "recipe," or "ingredients list" in certain industries.

BLANKET ORDER A long-term commitment to a vendor to purchase material, against which releases will be made for individual shipments. As a general rule, blanket orders are less flexible than vendor scheduling; they typically cover a specific quantity of one given item over a specific time period. Some blanket orders even have the individual shipment dates and quantities spelled out in advance.

BOILER PLATE A term used to describe the terms and conditions spelled out on the back side of a purchase order.

BUCKETED SYSTEM An MRP, DRP, or other time-phased system in which all time-phased data are accumulated into time periods or "buckets." If the period of accumulation would be one week, then the system would be said to have weekly buckets.

BUCKETLESS SYSTEM An MRP II, DRP, or other time-phased system in which all time-phased data are processed, stored, and displayed using dated records rather than defined time periods or "buckets."

BUSINESS PLAN A statement of income projections, costs, and profits usually accompanied by budgets and a projected balance sheet as well as a cash flow (source and application of funds) statement. It is usually stated in terms of dollars only. The business plan and the production plan, although frequently stated in different terms, should be in agreement with each other.

BUYER An individual whose functions may include vendor selection, negotiation, order release, vendor follow-up, measurement and control of vendor performance, value analysis, evaluation of new materials and processes, etc. In companies using vendor scheduling, the functions of order release and vendor follow-up are handled by the vendor scheduler, not the buyer.

BUYER/PLANNER A term sometimes used when the functions of buyer and vendor scheduler are combined into one job. Often used (imprecisely) as synonymous with planner/buyer or vendor scheduler.

CAPACITY BUYING A long-term commitment to a vendor to consume a given amount of his capacity per unit of time (for example, week, month). Schedules are then released periodically to the vendor in quantities to match the committed level of capacity. Capacity buying is somewhat less flexible than vendor scheduling, in that the committed levels of capacity typically must be "purchased" during each time period. Conceptually, capacity buying can be considered to fit between blanket ordering and vendor scheduling—more flexible than the former and less flexible than the latter.

CAPACITY REQUIREMENTS PLANNING (CRP)   The process of determining how much labor and/or machine resources are required to accomplish the tasks of production, and making plans to provide these resources. Open shop orders, as well as planned orders in the MRP system, are input to CRP, which "translates" these orders into hours of work by work center by time period. In earlier years, the computer portion of CRP was called "infinite loading," a misnomer.

CLOSED LOOP MRP   A system built around material requirements planning and also including the additional planning functions of production planning, master production scheduling, and capacity requirements planning. Further, once the planning phase is complete and the plans have been accepted as realistic and attainable, the execution functions come into play. These include the shop floor control functions of input/output measurement, dispatching, plus anticipated delay reports from both the shop and vendors, vendor scheduling, etc. The term "closed loop" implies that not only is each of these elements included in the overall system but also is each of these elements included in the overall system but also that there is feedback from the execution functions so that the planning can be kept valid at all times.

CONSIGNED STOCKS   Inventories of items which are in the possession of customers, dealers, agents, etc., but which remain the property of the supplier.

CONTRACT   An agreement between two or more competent parties to perform certain acts. A contract may be verbal or written. A purchase order, when accepted by a vendor, becomes a contract, as does a business agreement within the context of vendor scheduling.

CUMULATIVE LEAD TIME The longest length of time involved to accomplish the activity in question. For any item planned through MRP, it is found by reviewing each bill of material path below the item, and whichever path adds up to the greatest number defines cumulative material lead time. Also called aggregate lead time, stacked lead time, composite lead time, critical path lead time.

DELIVERY CYCLE The time between receipt of order and delivery of product.

DEMAND A need for a particular product or component. The demand could come from any number of sources—customer order, forecast, interplant, branch warehouse, service part—or to manufacture the next higher level. *See* dependent demand, independent demand.

DEMAND MANAGEMENT The function of recognizing and managing all of the demands for products to ensure that the master scheduler is aware of them. It encompasses the activities of forecasting, order entry, order promising, branch warehouse requirements, interplant requirements, interplant orders, and service parts requirements.

DEMONSTRATED CAPACITY Capacity calculated from actual performance data, usually number of items produced times standard hours per item.

DEPENDENT DEMAND Demand is considered dependent when it comes from production schedules for other items. These demands should be calculated, not forecasted. A given item may have both dependent and independent demand at any given time. *See* independent demand.

DIRECT MATERIALS Materials which become part of the finished product in measurable quantities.

DISPATCH LIST A listing of manufacturing orders in priority sequence according to the dispatching rules. The dispatch list is usually communicated to the manufacturing floor via hard copy or CRT display and contains detailed information on priority, location, quantity, and the capacity requirements of the manufacturing order by operation. Dispatch lists are normally generated daily and oriented by work center. Also called the "daily foremen's report."

DISPATCHING The selecting and sequencing of available jobs to be run at individual work stations and the assignment of these jobs to the workers.

DISTRIBUTION CENTER A warehouse with finished goods and/or service items. A typical company, for example, might have a manufacturing facility in Philadelphia and distribution centers in Atlanta, Dallas, Los Angeles, San Francisco, and Chicago. The term *distribution center* is synonymous with the term *branch warehouse*, although the former has become more commonly used recently. A warehouse that serves a group of satellite warehouses is usually called a regional distribution center.

DISTRIBUTION REQUIREMENTS PLANNING The function of determining the needs to replenish inventory at branch warehouses. A time-phased order-point approach is used, where the planned orders at the branch warehouse level are "exploded" via MRP logic to become gross requirements on the supplying source. In the case of multilevel distribution networks, this explosion process can continue down through the various levels of master warehouse, factory warehouse, etc., and become input to the master production schedule. Demand on the supplying source(s) is recognized as dependent, and standard MRP logic applies.

DISTRIBUTION RESOURCE PLANNING (DRP) The extension of Distribution Requirements Planning into the planning of the key resources contained in a distribution system: warehouse space, manpower, money, trucks and freight cars, etc.

DISTRIBUTOR A business which does not manufacture its own products, but rather purchases and resells products, usually out of a finished goods inventory.

DUE DATE The date when material is scheduled to be available.

FINAL ASSEMBLY SCHEDULE (FAS) Also referred to as the "finishing schedule," as it may include other operations than simply the final operation. It is a schedule of end items either to replenish finished goods inventory or to finish the product for a make-to-order product. For make-to-order products, it is prepared after receipt of a customer order, is constrained by the availability of material and capacity, and schedules the operations required to complete the product from the level where it is stocked (or master scheduled) to the end item level.

FINISHING LEAD TIME   The time needed to manufacture the product after receipt of the customer order.

FIRM PLANNED ORDER   A planned order that can be frozen in quantity and time. The computer is not allowed to change it; this is the responsibility of the planner in charge of the item. This technique can aid planners to respond to material and capacity problems by firming up selected planned orders. Firm planned orders are also the normal method of stating the master production schedule.

FIXED ORDER QUANTITY   An order quantity technique where the same quantity is planned to be ordered each time.

FLOW SHOP   A shop in which machines and operators handle a standard, usually uninterrupted material flow. The operators tend to perform the same operations for each production run. A flow shop is often referred to as a mass production shop, or is said to have a continuous manufacturing layout. The shop layout (arrangement of machines, benches, assembly lines, etc.) is designed to facilitate a product "flow." The process industries (chemicals, oil, paint, etc.) are extreme examples of flow shops. Each product, though variable in material specifications, uses the same flow pattern through the shop. *See* job shop.

F.O.B. (FREE ON BOARD)   This term means that the seller is required to place the goods aboard the equipment of the transporting carrier without cost to the buyer. In a contract, the "f.o.b." must be qualified by a name of a location, such as shipping point, destination, name of a city, mill, warehouse, etc. The stated f.o.b. point is usually the location where title to the goods passes from the seller to the buyer.

FULL PEGGING   Refers to the ability of a system to automatically trace requirements for a given component all the way up to its ultimate end item (or contract number).

GENERALLY ACCEPTED MANUFACTURING PRACTICES A group of practices and principles, independent of any one set of techniques, which defines how a manufacturing company should be managed. Included are such elements as the need for data accuracy, frequent communications between marketing and manufacturing, top management control of the production planning process, systems capable of validly translating high-level plans into detailed schedules, etc.

HEDGE 1. In purchasing, any purchase or sale transaction having as its purpose the elimination of the negative aspects of price fluctuations. 2. In master production scheduling, a quantity of stock used to protect against uncertainty in demand. The hedge is similar to safety stock, except that a hedge has the dimension of timing as well as amount.

HORIZONTAL DISPLAY A method of displaying output from an MRP system where requirements, scheduled receipts, projected balance, etc. are displayed horizontally, that is, across the page. Horizontal displays are difficult to use in conjunction with bucketless systems.

INDEPENDENT DEMAND Demand for an item is considered independent when such demand is unrelated to the demand for other items. Demand for finished goods and service parts are examples of independent demand.

INPUT/OUTPUT CONTROL A technique for capacity control where actual output from a work center is compared with the planned output (as developed by CRP and approved by manufacturing). The input is also monitored to see if it corresponds with plans so that work centers will not be expected to generate output when jobs are not available to work on.

INTERPLANT DEMAND Material to be shipped to another plant or division within the corporation. Although it is not a customer order, it is usually handled by the master production scheduling system in a similar manner.

INVENTORY TURNOVER The number of times that an inventory "turns over" or cycles during the year. One way to compute inventory turnover is to divide the average inventory level into the annual cost of sales. For example, if the average inventory were three million dollars and cost of sales were twenty-one million dollars, the inventory would be considered to turn over seven times per year.

ITEM RECORD The "master" record for an item. Typically it contains identifying and descriptive data, control values (lead times, lot order quantities, etc.) and may contain data on inventory status, requirements, and planned orders. Item records are linked together by bill of material records (or product structure records), thus defining the bill of material.

JOB SHOP A functional organization whose departments or work centers are organized around particular types of equipment or operations, such as drilling, forging, spinning, or assembly. Products move through departments by individual shop orders.

JUST-IN-TIME In the narrow sense, a method of execution designed to result in minimum inventory by having material arrive at each operation just in time to be used. In the broad sense, it refers to all the activities of manufacturing which make the Just-in-Time movement of material possible, with the ultimate goal being elimination of waste. Just-in-Time is possible via MRP II or, in some cases, via Kanban.

KANBAN A scheduling approach which uses standard containers with a card attached to each. Developed in Japan, it has been used in certain highly repetitive manufacturing environments to achieve Just-in-Time. Kanban in Japanese loosely translated means "card," literally "billboard" or "sign."

LEAD TIME A span of time required to perform an activity. In a logistics context, the activity in question is normally the procurement of materials and/or products either from an outside supplier or one's own manufacturing facility. The individual components of any given lead time can include some or all or the following: order preparation time, queue time, move or transportation time, receiving and inspection time.

LEAD TIME OFFSET A term used in MRP where a planned order receipt in one time period will require the release of that order in some earlier time period based on the lead time for the item.

The difference between the due date and the release date is the lead time offset.

LOAD The amount of scheduled work ahead of a manufacturing facility, usually expressed in terms of hours of work or units of production.

LOGISTICS In an industrial context, this term refers to the functions of obtaining and distributing material and product. In a military sense (where it has greater usage), its meaning can also include the transportation of personnel.

LOT-FOR-LOT An order quantity technique in MRP which generates planned orders in quantities equal to the net requirements in each period. Also called discrete, one-for-one.

MAINTENANCE REPAIR AND OPERATING SUPPLIES (MRO) Items used in support of general operations and maintenance such as spare parts, maintenance supplies, consumables used in the manufacturing process, etc.

MAKE-TO-ORDER PRODUCT A product which is finished after receipt of a customer order. Frequently, long lead time components are planned prior to the order arriving in order to reduce the delivery time to the customer. Where options or other subassemblies are stocked prior to customer orders arriving, the term "assemble-to-order" is frequently used.

MAKE-TO-STOCK PRODUCT A product intended to be shipped from the finished goods inventory "off the shelf" and which therefore is finished prior to a customer order arriving.

MANUFACTURING RESOURCE PLANNING (MRP II) A method for the effective planning of all resources of a manufacturing company. Ideally, it addresses operational planning in units, financial planning in dollars, and has a simulation capability to answer "what if" questions. It is made up of a variety of functions, each linked together: business planning, production planning, master production scheduling, material requirements planning, capacity requirements planning, and the execution support systems for capacity and material. Output from these systems would be integrated with financial reports such as the business plan, purchase commitment reports, shipping budget, inventory projections in dollars, etc. Manufacturing Resource Planning is a direct out-growth and extension of closed loop MRP. MRP II has also been defined, validly, as a management system based on network scheduling. Also, and perhaps best, as organized common sense.

MASTER PRODUCTION SCHEDULE (MPS) The anticipated build schedule. The master scheduler maintains this schedule and, in turn, it becomes a set of planning numbers which "drives" MRP. It represents what the company plans to produce expressed in specific configurations, quantities, and dates. The master pro-duction schedule must take into account customer orders and forecasts, backlog, availability of material, availability of capacity, management policy and goals, etc.

MASTER SCHEDULE ITEM An item number selected to be planned by the master scheduler. The item would be deemed critical in terms of its impact on lower-level components and/or resources such as skilled labor, key machines, dollars, etc. Therefore, the master scheduler, not the computer, would maintain the plan for these items. A master schedule item may be an end item, a com-ponent, a pseudo number, or a planning bill of material.

MASTER SCHEDULER The job title of the person who manages the master production schedule. This person should have sub-stantial knowledge of the company's products, processes, and people.

MATERIAL REQUIREMENTS PLANNING (MRP) A set of techniques which uses bills of material, inventory data, and the master pro-duction schedule to calculate requirements for materials. It makes recommendations to release replenishment orders for material. Further, since it is time phased, it makes recommendations to reschedule open orders when due dates and need dates are not in phase. Originally seen as merely a better way to order inven-tory, today it is thought of primarily as a scheduling technique—that is, a method for establishing and maintaining valid due dates on orders. It is the foundation for closed loop MRP.

MATERIAL REVIEW BOARD (MRB) An organization within a com-pany, often a standing committee, which has the job of determining the disposition of items which have questionable quality or other attributes.

MATERIALS MANAGEMENT An organizational structure which groups the functions related to the complete cycle of material flow, from the purchase and internal control of production materials to the planning and control of work-in-process to the warehousing, shipping, and distribution of the finished product.

MURPHY'S LAW A tongue-in-cheek observation which states: "If anything can go wrong, it will."

NEED DATE The date when an item is required for its intended use. *See* due date.

NET CHANGE MRP A method of processing material requirements planning on the computer whereby the material plan is continually retained in the computer. Whenever there is a change in requirements, open order or inventory status, bills of material, etc., a partial explosion is made only for those parts affected by the change.

NET REQUIREMENTS In MRP, the net requirements for a part or an assembly are derived as a result of netting gross requirements against inventory on hand and the scheduled receipts. Net requirements, lot sized and offset for lead time, become planned orders.

ON-HAND BALANCE The quantity shown in the inventory records as being physically in stock.

OPEN ORDER An active manufacturing order or purchase order. Also called scheduled receipts.

ORDER ENTRY The process of accepting and translating what a customer wants into terms used by the manufacturer. This can be as simple as creating shipping documents for a finished goods product to a far more complicated series of activities including engineering effort for make-to-order products.

ORDER PROMISING The process of making a delivery commitment, that is, answering the question "When can you ship?" For make-to-order products, this usually involves a check of material and capacity availability.

ORDER QUANTITY The amount of an item to be ordered. Also called lot size.

PAPERLESS PURCHASING A purchasing operation which does not employ purchase requisitions or hard-copy purchase orders. In actual practice, usually a small amount of paper is used, normally in the form of the vendor schedule. Transmitting the vendor schedule electronically would result in a totally paperless operation.

PEGGING In MRP, pegging displays, for a given item, the details of the sources of its gross requirements and/or allocations. Pegging can be thought of as "live" where-used information.

PERIOD ORDER QUANTITY An order quantity technique under which the order quantity will be equal to the net requirements for a given number of periods (for example, weeks) into the future. Also called days' supply, weeks' supply, fixed period.

PLANNED ORDER A suggested order quantity and due date created by MRP processing, when it encounters net requirements. Planned orders are created by the computer, exist only within the computer, and may be changed or deleted by the computer during subsequent MRP processing if conditions change. Planned orders at one level will be exploded into gross requirements for components at the next lower level. Planned orders also serve as input to capacity requirements planning, along with scheduled receipts, to show the total capacity requirements in future time periods.

PLANNER/BUYER See vendor scheduler.

PRICE BREAK A lower unit price offered by a vendor for a larger quantity order. This enables the vendor to apply order processing and setup costs over a larger production run. The advantage to the customer is lower unit cost; the disadvantage can be higher inventories.

PRICE PREVAILING AT DATE OF SHIPMENT An agreement between the purchaser and the vendor that the price of the goods ordered is subject to change at the vendor's discretion between the date of order and the date of shipment.

PRODUCTION PLANNING The function of setting the overall level of manufacturing output. Its prime purpose is to establish production rates that will achieve management's objective in terms of raising or lowering inventories or backlogs, while usually attempting to keep the production force relatively stable. The production plan is usually stated in broad terms (e.g., product groupings, families of products). It must extend through a planning horizon sufficient to plan the labor, equipment, facilities, material, and finances required to accomplish the production plan. Various units of measure are used by different companies to express the plan such as standard hours, tonnage, labor operators, units, pieces, etc. As this plan affects all company functions, it is normally prepared with information from marketing, manufacturing, engineering, finance, materials, etc. In turn, the production plan becomes management's authorization for the master scheduler to convert into a more detailed plan.

PROGRESS PAYMENTS   Payments in advance of delivery for certain amounts or percentages of the purchase price, usually based on work completed.

PROJECTED AVAILABLE BALANCE   The inventory balance projected out into the future. It is the running sum of on-hand inventory, minus requirements, plus scheduled receipts and (usually) planned orders.

PURCHASE ORDER   The purchaser's document used to formalize a purchase transaction with a vendor. A purchase order typically contains statements of items, description, quantity and price; terms of payment, performance and transportation; and other terms and conditions.

PURCHASE REQUISITION   The communication link between the person who knows the need for an item and the people who are in direct contact with the vendor, typically the purchasing department. In many companies, the purchase requisition is considered as the authorization to buy.

QUEUE   A waiting line. In manufacturing, the jobs at a given work center waiting to be processed. As queues increase, so do average lead times and work-in-process inventories.

QUEUE TIME   The amount of time a job waits at a work center before setup or work is performed on the job. Queue time is one element of total manufacturing lead time. Increases in queue time result in direct increases to manufacturing lead time.

QUOTATION A bid; a statement of price, terms of sale, and description of goods or services offered by a vendor to a prospective purchaser.

REGENERATION MRP A method of processing material requirements planning on the computer whereby the master production schedule is totally reexploded down through all bills of material, at least once per week to maintain valid priorities. New requirements and planned orders are completely "regenerated" at that time.

REPETITIVE MANUFACTURING Production of discrete units, planned and executed via schedule, usually at relatively high speeds and volumes. Material tends to move in a sequential flow. *See flow shop.*

RESCHEDULING ASSUMPTION A fundamental piece of MRP logic which assumes that existing open orders can be rescheduled in nearer time periods far more easily than new orders can be released and received. As a result, planned order receipts are not created until all scheduled receipts have been applied to cover gross requirements.

ROUGH-CUT CAPACITY PLANNING The process of converting the production plan and/or the master production schedule into capacity needs for key resources: manpower, machinery, warehouse space, vendors' capabilities, and in some cases, money. Product load profiles are often used to accomplish this. The purpose of rough-cut capacity planning is to evaluate the plan prior to attempting to implement it. Sometimes called resource requirements planning.

ROUTING A document detailing the manufacture of a particular item. It includes the operations to be performed, their sequence, the various work centers to be involved, and the standards for setup and run. In some companies, the routing also includes information on tooling, operator skill levels, inspection operations, testing requirements, etc.

SAFETY STOCK In general, a quantity of stock planned to be available to protect against fluctuations in demand and/or supply.

SAFETY TIME A technique in MRP whereby material is planned to arrive ahead of the requirement date. The difference between the requirement date and the planned in-stock-date is safety time.

SCHEDULED RECEIPTS Within MRP, open production orders and open purchase orders are considered as "scheduled receipts" on their due date and will be treated as part of available inventory during the netting process for the time period in question. Scheduled receipt dates and/or quantities are not normally altered automatically by the computer. Further, scheduled receipts are not exploded into requirements for components, as MRP logic assumes that all components required for the manufacture of the item in question have either been allocated or issued to the shop floor.

SCRAP FACTOR A percentage factor used by MRP to increase gross requirements of a given component to account for anticipated loss of that component during the manufacture of its parent.

SERVICE PARTS Parts used for the repair and/or maintenance of a product. Also called repair parts, spares.

SHOP FLOOR CONTROL A system for utilizing data from the shop floor as well as data processing files to maintain and communicate status information on shop orders (manufacturing orders) and work centers. The major subfunctions of shop floor control are: (1) assigning priority of each shop order; (2) maintaining work-in-process quantity information; (3) conveying shop order status information; (4) providing actual input and output data for capacity control purposes; (5) providing quantity by location by shop order for work-in-process inventory and accounting purposes; and (6) providing measurement of efficiency, utilization, and productivity of manpower and machines.

SHRINKAGE FACTOR A factor used in material requirements planning which compensates for expected loss during the manufacturing cycle either by increasing the gross requirements or by reducing the expected completion quantity of planned and open orders. The shrinkage factor differs from the scrap factor in that the former affects all uses of the part and its components. The scrap relates to only one usage.

SIMULATION Within MRP II, utilizing the operational data to perform "what-if" evaluations of alternative plans, to answer the question "Can we do it?" If yes, the simulation can then be run in financial mode to help answer the question "Do we really want to?"

SOURCE INSPECTION Inspection at the source (e.g., the vendor) instead of inspecting following receipt of the items.

STOCKLESS PURCHASING Buying parts and supplies for direct utilization by the departments involved, as opposed to receiving them into stores and subsequently issuing them to the departments.

TIME BUCKET A number of days of data summarized into one columnar display. A weekly time bucket in MRP would contain all of the relevant planning data for an entire week. Weekly time buckets are considered to be the largest possible (at least in the near and medium term) to permit effective MRP.

TIME FENCE Point in time where various restrictions or changes in operating procedures take place. For example, changes to the master production schedule can be accomplished easily beyond the cumulative lead time, whereas changes inside the cumulative lead time become increasingly more difficult, to a point where changes should be resisted. Time fences can be used to define these points.

VENDOR SCHEDULER A person whose main job is working with vendors regarding what's needed and when. Vendor schedulers are in direct contact with both MRP and the vendors. They do the material planning for the items under their control, communicate the resultant schedules to their assigned vendors, do follow-up, resolve problems, etc. The vendor schedulers are normally organized by commodity, as are the buyers. By using the vendor scheduler approach, the buyers are freed from day-to-day order placement and expediting, and therefore, have the time to do cost reduction, negotiation, vendor selection, alternate sourcing, etc. Another term for vendor scheduler is planner/buyer.

VENDOR SCHEDULING A purchasing approach which provides vendors with schedules rather than individual hard-copy purchase orders. Normally, a vendor scheduling system will include a business agreement (contract) for each vendor, a weekly schedule for each vendor extending for some time into the future, and individuals called vendor schedulers. Also required is a formal priority planning system that works very well, because it is essential in this arrangement to provide the vendor with valid due dates routinely.

WORK-IN-PROCESS Product in various stages of completion throughout the plant, including raw material that has been released for initial processing and completely processed material awaiting final inspection and acceptance as finished product or shipment to a customer. Many accounting systems also include semifinished stock and components in this category.

ZERO INVENTORIES A term adopted by APICS (American Production and Inventory Control Society), the meaning of which is similar to Just-in-Time.

Index